WORSHIP
THE LORD
IN PRAYER

WORSHIP THE LORD IN PRAYER

John H. Gomes

Covenant Temple
36 Hunts Brook Road
Quaker Hill, CT 06320 (USA)

ABOUT THE COVER

The cover illustration represents two periods of time:
something from days of old and also something new.

*Matthew 13:52 ~ Then He said to them, "Therefore every scribe
instructed concerning the kingdom of heaven is like a householder
who brings out of his treasure things new and old."*

The old: the altar of incense
(the smoke of burning incense was symbolic of praise)

Exodus 30:1 ~ "You shall make an altar to burn incense on."

The new: the depiction within the altar
(the live sacrifice of praise; the fruit offered by the lips of the people)

*Hebrews 13:15 ~ "Therefore by Him let us continually offer the sacrifice of
praise to God, that is, the fruit of our lips, giving thanks to His name."*

*This book is especially dedicated as a refreshing
to those who stood and fought,
to the battle worn,
who did not abandon their hope.
It is also dedicated to those who have given up,
as a true encouragement
to help with the restoration of their hope.*

ACKNOWLEDGEMENTS

With heartfelt thanksgiving I would like to express my gratitude
to the Lord Jesus for giving me the privilege to share with
His people how truly worthy He is to be praised.

I would also like to thankfully acknowledge the
following people who willingly gave of themselves, their time,
and talents in support of this work.

Deborah Ann Brigante, Senior Editor
Meg Jacobs, Assistant Editor
Jennifer Gomes, Cover Design
Hector Rodriguez, Interior Illustrations
Angela Ciccone, Typist

*...the whole body, joined and knit together by what every joint supplies,
according to the effective working by which every part does its share,
causes growth of the body for the edifying of itself in love.*

Ephesians 4:16

ABOUT THE AUTHOR

John Gomes was born and raised in Aruba, an island territory of the Netherlands. Despite being challenged by dyslexia, a non-intellectual learning disability that made it difficult for him to communicate his thoughts, both verbally and on paper, he became one of the island's most respected businessmen. As he was preparing to embark on a new business venture, one that was sure to increase his already substantial wealth, he heard from the Lord. The Lord called John to leave behind all of his worldly works and instead to invest all of his focus on becoming a disciple of His Word.

After several years of study in Aruba, Pastor John, his wife, Stella, and their three young children moved to the United States. He continued his studies in the States, and in 1991 was offered the position of an assistant pastor, a role he accepted without curtailing his studies. In 1994, Pastor John was led by the Holy Spirit to start his own church; hence, Covenant Temple (a church based on praise, prayer, and restoration) was established.

In spite of his ordainment, Pastor John's love for the Word, and his desire to care for his sheep, motivates him to continue his daily studies of the Bible. Along with shepherding his own church, Pastor John has conducted Pastors and Leaders conferences on four continents. He has, by his God-given ability to explain God's Word, authored books and study guides that have helped numerous people around the world to easily understand and find freedom in the Word of God. Since his life changing decision to heed the voice of the Lord, Pastor John has gone from amassing wealth as a businessman to becoming a servant of the Lord helping countless in the body of Christ to live truly victorious lives.

TABLE OF CONTENTS

INTRODUCTION

FINDING A CONFIDENCE GOD HEARS

The most precious thing that Christians possess is their faith, their assured belief in the existence of God. Every time we pray we are putting our faith into action. Why does it seem that our faith is so often not enough to allow us to possess the genuine confidence that God truly hears us when we pray? There can be many answers to that question but there is only one true remedy; we need to wholeheartedly believe in the truthfulness of God's Word. We need to grasp with certainty what is written in the Bible.

> **1 John 5:14-15** Now this is the confidence that we have in Him, that if we ask anything according to His will, He hears us. And if we know that He hears us, whatever we ask, we know that we have the petitions that we have asked of Him.

In order to thoroughly grasp that verse, we need to take a closer look at our prayers. Are you one of the countless people who question whether or not your prayers are being heard? Do you ask yourself, *Why have I prayed more than once about a certain matter and have not (yet) been answered?* Do you question if the prayers of others, especially those of leaders, carry more weight before God than yours? And if you are questioning whether or not God is a respecter of the prayer petitioner, are you also questioning if your prayers merit God's favor? If you have any of these questions, how can it be possible to completely trust that it is the will of God to meet all of your needs and to answer every prayer that you lift in the name of Jesus.

God hears everyone's prayers; no one is more favored or special. God refers to the prophet Elijah as possessing a nature like ours (James 5:17). He was a simple man who served the Lord, he also had to deal with fears, doubts, and weaknesses, which you can read about in 1 Kings 17-19. When we allow fear or doubt to influence the words of our prayers we are limiting their power. We are displaying a lack of confidence, which is the very thing the Word tells us is so important to possess.

I was at one time among those who were not always confident that God heard me when I prayed. There were times, during my years of service as an assistant pastor, when leading the church in prayer seemed tedious and difficult. I am so thankful that I serve a merciful God. He patiently spent time with me, ministering to my soul and revealing to me why I lacked the assurance that I was in His will. He brought to light why I was having difficulty receiving answers to my prayers. He showed me when we allow fear or doubt to influence the words of our prayers, we are undermining our belief that our prayers will be heard. Instead, we must present our prayers boldly, forthrightly, with a plainspoken frankness, and believe that not only will our prayers be heard, but they will be answered as well. He shared with me how precious everyone's prayers are to Him. God was faithful to hear and answer Elijah's prayers and He will do the same for all who call on His name.

CHAPTER ONE

WORSHIP THE LORD IN PRAYER

W orshiping the Lord in prayer is not a new concept. It is a commandment that was ordained with His introduction to the Israelites, at the time of their deliverance from Egypt. However, it is as relevant today as it was then. When we worship the Lord we are expressing, through prayers and/or songs, our love for Him. David worshiped the Lord in prayer; this is evidenced in the Book of Psalms. David authored most of the psalms, many as individual prayers presented to God in the form of a song (praise). As we read Psalm 18:3, "I will call upon the LORD, *who is worthy* to be praised; So shall I be saved from my enemies," we can clearly see that three separate actions are emphasized:

- calling on the Lord—to pray, petition, beseech
- praising the Lord—to acknowledge His goodness
- being saved—to be delivered, rescued, set free

Perhaps the most significant action in the verse is the one that is not written; it is the confidence that David displays when he proclaims, *I will call, praise, and I will be saved.* David trusted that when he called on (prayed to) the Lord and praised (worshiped) Him, that the Lord would surely hear him and save him whenever the need arose.

David called upon the Lord not only when he had a need but continually. At times he called upon the Lord solely to praise Him, because David knew the Lord was worthy and deserving of praise. David also knew that he would have an ongoing need to be saved from his enemies, so with thanksgiving in his heart and praise on his lips he worshiped the Lord continually. David truly found the grace of God and trustfully tapped into it as often as the need arose because he knew he served a merciful God. He was a man after God's own heart, not because of who he was or anything he had done, but simply because he knew he served a gracious God in whose mercies he could forever trust.

David's practice of worshiping the Lord and his desire to obey the Word of God was his passion. David developed an intimate relationship with the Lord through praise and prayer. He possessed a strong confidence (a peace that surpasses understanding that God always hears) that he would be saved (delivered) from all his enemies. David understood just how important praise (thanksgiving) was in cultivating a confidence in a successful prayer relationship with God. When we praise God continually we are repeatedly declaring His goodness, His faithfulness, and His tender mercies. This not only exalts and glorifies Him, it also reinforces (strengthens) our confidence in His willingness to keep His promises (Word). Praise is the key component, necessary to deliver us from doubts concerning God's desire to answer the prayers of all His people.

CHAPTER TWO

PRAISE IS THANKSGIVING

Praise is the most excellent form of thanksgiving we can offer the Lord. Praise glorifies the Lord and it also benefits those who do so; it brings peace to their hearts and minds. Our prayer requests should always be presented with praise. Praise God before you lift your petition to Him. Praise Him with songs that declare He is a good and merciful God. Present your prayer and continue to praise Him while you are waiting to see your prayer answered, because by faith, you know you already have the answer to your prayer. The Lord revealed that the simplest expression of our faith is to give thanks, before and after prayer, and the most beautiful form of thanks is to praise Him in song.

David's petitions (prayers) were always lifted to the Lord accompanied by praise. The Holy Spirit, with great seriousness, asks God's people to present their prayers mixed with praise.

> **Philippians 4:4-7** Rejoice in the Lord always. Again I will say, rejoice! Let your gentleness be known to all men. The Lord *is* at hand. (6)Be anxious for nothing, but in everything by prayer and supplication, with

thanksgiving, let your requests be made known to God; and the peace of God, which surpasses all understanding, will guard your hearts and minds through Christ Jesus.

These verses tell us to "rejoice in the Lord always" because He is always at hand. He is closer than a brother and He will never leave us or forsake (abandon, desert) us. We need not worry about anything. When we pray in times of trouble, with thanksgiving on our lips, the peace of God will guard our hearts and minds.

God's Word encourages us to give Him thanks in all things. Many of us think that a simple and sincere, *Thank You, Lord,* at the close of our prayers is what Philippians 4:6 is referring to; some even think that it is acceptable to wait until they see the answer to their prayer manifested before giving thanks to the Lord. But in truth, God wants us to envelop our prayers and petitions with praise (thanksgiving). We should offer up praise before we pray, in the midst of our prayers, and at the close of our prayers. When we give thanks before we see the answer to our prayers, we are declaring our confidence (trust, faith) in a merciful God who is faithful to provide all of our needs.

Practice thanking Him in all situations. We become proficient at the things we invest time in, to practice. Read Romans 8:31-32 slowly/deliberately, so that you may truly grasp it, and begin to wholeheartedly thank Him.

Romans 8:31-32 What then shall we say to these things? If God *is* for us, who *can be* against us? He who did not spare His own Son, but delivered Him up for us all, how shall He not with Him also freely give us all things?

In these verses, the Lord is questioning our faith; He is questioning our willingness to believe that it is His desire to meet (provide) all of our needs. These verses simply ask us to consider that if God loved us enough to willingly sacrifice His only Son for our sakes, then how much more does He desire to freely give us all things.

CHAPTER THREE

INCENSE IS SYMBOLIC OF PRAISE

In the Bible, incense is symbolic of praise. We can clearly see the importance of praise accompanying prayers when we look at the Book of Revelation. Here, God Himself provides us with this perfect example of how our prayers should be enveloped in a cloud of burning incense so that they may ascend before Him.

> **Revelation 8:3-4** Then another angel, having a golden censer, came and stood at the altar. He was given much incense, that he should offer *it* with the prayers of all the saints upon the golden altar which was before the throne. And the smoke of the incense, with the prayers of the saints, ascended before God from the angel's hand.

The high priest would burn incense created by a perfumer, who extracted the moisture from a compound of the following sweet spices: stacte, onycha, galbanum, and frankincense of equal amounts. When the extracted moisture was dried, it crystallized. The crystals (stones) would then be crushed into a very fine powder (incense). Jesus requires praise from His people; if we choose to stop praising Him with the sounds of our lips, stones (incense) will praise Him. "I tell you that if these should keep silent, the stones would immediately cry out" (Luke 19:40). Would you want a stone, a lifeless object, to praise the One who gave you life in your place? Today we no longer burn incense; it is the joyful sounds of our lips, our praises that the Lord requires. Sadly however, so many have returned to the religious attitude of burning incense in place of lifting praises with their voices.

The significance of burning incense and offering it up to the Lord before lifting prayer petitions can be traced back to the time when the Israelites wandered through the wilderness. God desired a place where He could meet with His people, so He gave Moses specific instructions concerning how to build the tabernacle. The tabernacle was often referred to as the "tent of meeting." In fact, it was a portable sanctuary, which could be moved from place to place as often as the people relocated their camp.

The tent of meeting was comprised of three main areas, the courtyard, the outer room (the Holy Place), and the inner room (the Holy of Holies, or the Most Holy Place). The largest of these, the courtyard, was a rectangular shaped area enclosed by a fence. The tabernacle was placed in the rear westward side of the courtyard. The courtyard also contained the altar used to sacrifice animals and the laver where the priest washed himself before putting on the garments that were required to safely enter the tabernacle.

The Holy Place, the larger of the tabernacle's interior spaces, housed the table of showbread and the golden lampstand. The Holy Place was separated from the Holy of Holies by a veil that spanned from the floor to the ceiling. The Holy of Holies was the most sacred place of all, only the high priest was permitted (by God) to enter it. It contained the altar of incense and the ark of the covenant (also referred to as the ark of the Lord or the ark of the Testimony). It was here that the high priest would bring the incense offering, twice daily before the Lord, in preparation for the presentation of prayers. Additionally, he would offer a blood offering within the Holy of Holies, once each year, on the Day of Atonement, as a covering for sins.

Consider the contents of the tabernacle, specifically the altar of incense, described in Exodus 30:1-10. Pay special attention to the purpose (function) of the altar of incense in verses 7-10:

> **Exodus 30:1-10** "You shall make an altar to burn incense on; you shall make it of acacia wood. "A cubit *shall be* its length and a cubit its width—it shall be square—and two cubits *shall be* its height. Its horns *shall be* of one piece with it. "And you shall overlay its top, its sides all around, and its horns with pure gold; and you shall make for it a molding of gold all around. "Two gold rings you shall make for it, under the molding on both its sides. You shall place *them* on its two sides, and they will be holders for the poles with which to bear it. "You shall make the poles of acacia wood, and overlay them with gold. "And you shall put it before the veil that *is* before the ark of the Testimony, before the mercy seat that *is* over the Testimony, where I will meet with you. (7)"Aaron shall burn on it sweet incense every morning; when he tends the lamps, he shall burn incense on it. "And when Aaron lights the lamps at twilight, he shall burn incense on it, a perpetual incense before the Lord throughout your generations. "You shall not offer strange incense on it, or a burnt offering, or a grain offering; nor shall you pour a drink offering on it. "And Aaron shall make atonement upon its horns once a year with the

blood of the sin offering of atonement; once a year he shall make atonement upon it throughout your generations. It *is* most holy to the LORD."

The Lord gave specific instructions that the ark (Exodus 25:12), the table (Exodus 25:26), and the altar of sacrifice (Exodus 27:4) were all to be constructed with four rings. However, the Lord instructed that the *altar of incense* was to be constructed with *two* rings under its crown (top). Many believe that it was constructed with four rings and that the staves (rods) were passed through the four rings for the purpose of carrying the altar. This is a common misconception because the altar of incense is so often portrayed as having four rings. The instructions God gave Moses clearly stated that *two* rings were to be attached at the altar's furthest diagonal corners. "And two golden rings shalt thou make to it under the crown of it, by the two corners thereof, upon the two **sides** of it shalt thou make it; and they shall be for places for the staves to bear it withal" (Exodus 30:4 KJV). The word "sides" is translated from the Hebrew word *tsad*, and is defined as: sidle off (to move sideways); figuratively speaking, an adversary (example: the two furthest opposite corners).

It is believed by consensus, that the altar of incense was placed inside the Holy Place, and that it was positioned in front of the veil that separated the Holy Place from the Holy of Holies. This is a misinterpretation; in truth, the altar of incense was placed *inside* the Holy of Holies, *behind* the veil that separated the Holy Place from the Holy of Holies, and it was positioned *before* the ark of the Testimony. If you do a study on the *Day of Atonement*, you will have difficulty with the depiction of the golden altar's placement in the Holy Place because if this widely accepted belief is true, how then could it have been possible for the cloud of incense to cover the mercy seat? The veil that separated the Holy Place from the Holy of Holies would have contained the cloud of incense in the Holy Place, making that impossible. **See the illustration below.**

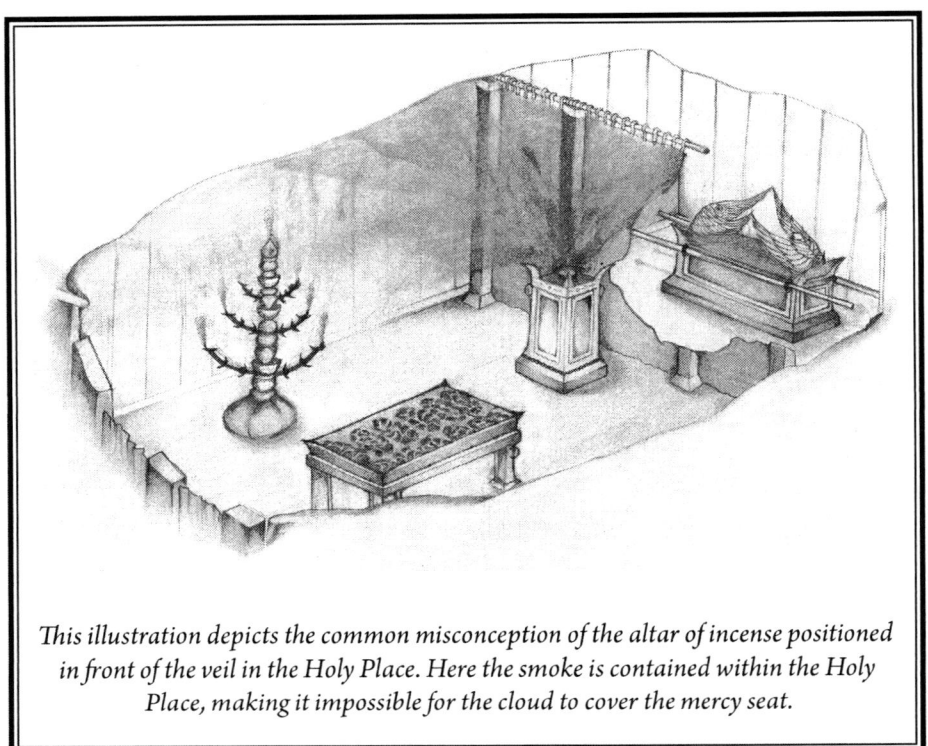

This illustration depicts the common misconception of the altar of incense positioned in front of the veil in the Holy Place. Here the smoke is contained within the Holy Place, making it impossible for the cloud to cover the mercy seat.

In Leviticus, the Lord tells Moses to strongly warn Aaron that approaching the mercy seat when it is not covered by the cloud of incense will result in his death:

> **Leviticus 16:2,13** …and the LORD said to Moses: "Tell Aaron your brother not to come at *just* any time into the Holy *Place* inside the veil, before the mercy seat which *is* on the ark, lest he die; for I will appear in the cloud above the mercy seat. "And he shall put the incense on the fire before the LORD, **that the cloud of incense may cover the mercy seat that *is* on the Testimony,** lest he die.

When we read Exodus 30:7-8, we see that the Lord instructed Aaron to burn incense twice a day, each morning and again each evening. This would assure that there would be a covering of incense on the mercy seat, in preparation for the priests who would bring the prayers of the people before the Lord for answers and continual guidance on their behalf.

> **Exodus 25:22** "And there I will meet with you, and I will speak with you from above the mercy seat, from between the two cherubim which *are* on the ark of the Testimony, about everything which I will give you in commandment to the children of Israel.

When we look at Exodus 30:36, "And you shall beat *some* of it very fine, and put some of it **before the Testimony** in the tabernacle of meeting **where I will meet with you**. It shall be most holy to you," we find additional confirmation that the Lord created a place to *meet* with the priests, *before* the Testimony (mercy seat). It was common practice for the Israelites to bring, or to have the priests bring, their prayers before the Lord during the burning of incense; they continued to do so even up to the time of Jesus. "And the whole multitude of the people was praying outside at the hour of incense" (Luke 1:10).

I was, at one time, among those who believed that the altar of incense was in the Holy Place. However, there came a time when the Lord brought me to Hebrews 9:1-4, and He showed me where it is written that the altar of incense was located in the Holy of Holies. (This exact placement of the articles described in the Book of Hebrews is also confirmed in all well-known translations.) I immediately accepted this revelation but I struggled as I tried to confirm it in the Old Testament; what I had seen written there seemed contrary to what was written in the New Testament.

Thank God for the assurance we have that His Word does **not** contradict itself. It was that assurance that kept me faithful with my quest to grasp what the Lord was attempting to reveal to me. I would read Exodus, over and over again, and I would actually find myself arguing with the Lord. What He revealed to me seemed to differ from what I had been casually reading. Each time I read about the construction and the placement of the altar of incense, in Exodus 30 and Exodus 40, it seemed clear to me that the altar was placed outside the veil, in the Holy Place.

> **Hebrews 9:1-4a** Then indeed, even the first *covenant* had ordinances of divine service and the earthly sanctuary. For a tabernacle was prepared: the first *part*, in which *was* the lampstand, the table, and the showbread, which is called the sanctuary; and behind the second veil, the part of the tabernacle which is called the Holiest of All, which had the **golden censer** and the ark of the covenant overlaid on all sides with gold...

My inability to grasp what the Lord was showing me continued for almost two years. Thank God for His mercy and His patience. One day the Lord asked me to look more carefully at the words I was reading; I could feel His displeasure. His anger was kindled towards me because during this period of time, I was not placing enough importance on what He was trying to show me. He had to repeatedly bring me back to resume my studies of this subject. The more diligently I examined the words the Lord used to describe where the articles of the tabernacle were to be placed, the clearer the truth became. My difficulty in grasping what He was trying to reveal to me was due to the error/inaccuracy that I was taught to believe as truth. Once you have been taught something and believe it to be the truth, it can be extremely difficult to accept change.

This difficulty can open the door for the enemy to cause stubbornness and rejection of the truth, just as it did to the Bible scholars of Jesus' day. They were blinded by the false teachings that they had come to believe and accept as the truth. Their flawed understanding of the truth caused them to reject Jesus and Christianity. They built walls around their erroneous knowledge. They would not allow anyone to penetrate them with the truth, not even the Lord who presented them with a true and clear understanding of His Word, to deliver them from incorrect knowledge (hearsay).

> **John 12:38-40** …that the word of Isaiah the prophet might be fulfilled, which he spoke: *"Lord, who has believed our report? And to whom has the arm of the LORD been revealed?"* Therefore they could not believe, because Isaiah said again: *"He has blinded their eyes and hardened their hearts, Lest they should see with their eyes, Lest they should understand with their hearts and turn, So that I should heal them."*

Paul and Silas faced this same situation when they preached that 'Jesus is the Christ' in a Jewish synagogue in Berea. The Jewish leaders present at that time had a decision to make. Would they reject this revelation and continue to hold on to what they had been taught, and believed to be the truth, or would they search the Scriptures seeking proof that would either confirm or disprove what they were hearing? They chose the latter, and in doing so their eyes as well as those of many of their followers/attendants were opened to the truth. They confirmed Paul and Silas' preaching in God's Word and they were then able to pass the revelation on, fulfilling their responsibility to their followers. The Bible referred to them as fair-minded (more noble) because they did not quickly reject knowledge but instead, for their benefit and for that of their followers, they diligently searched the Scriptures to verify if the things they were hearing were true. We have this same responsibility today.

> **Acts 17:11-12** These were more fair-minded than those in Thessalonica, in that they received the word with all readiness, and searched the Scriptures daily *to find out* whether these things were so. Therefore many of them believed, and also not a few of the Greeks, prominent women as well as men.

The origin of Christianity can be traced to Judaism; it began as a fragment of the Jewish faith. Initially, only a small number embraced the teachings of Jesus but as newcomers (new believers, gentiles) were drawn to Jesus, its numbers increased. We can see evidence of this when we read Acts 19:1-10. This trend (fragmentation) continued down through the centuries. The church was fragmented as the Holy Spirit used different protesters such as Martin Luther (1483-1546), Huldrych Zwingli (1484-1531), and John Calvin (1509-1564), to rekindle the fires in the church for truth; thus, we have the denominations that exist today. There were others as well, such as John Wesley, and his brother Charles, who founded the Methodist denomination. The Pentecostal movement was one of the most recent fragmentations of the church.

Today, as a result of the walls the general church built around their understanding, they could not accept the outpouring, the baptism of the Holy Spirit, along with the evidence of speaking in tongues. The Holy Spirit continually wants to increase our understanding of the Word of God. To benefit from that increase, we must keep an open and sensitive heart. Pray. Ask the Lord to open your eyes. Search the Scriptures, seeking confirmation.

In Exodus 26:33-35, the Lord used specific words to describe precisely how the veil was to be hung and where the ark of the Testimony, the table of showbread, and the golden lampstand were to be placed:

> **Exodus 26:33-35 KJV** And thou shalt hang up the veil under the taches, that thou mayest bring in thither **within** the veil the ark of the testimony: and the veil shall divide unto you between the holy *place* and the most holy. And thou shalt put the mercy seat upon the ark of the testimony in the most holy *place*. And thou shalt set the table **without** the veil, and the candlestick over against the table on the side of the tabernacle toward the south: and thou shalt put the table on the north side.

In the Hebrew language, the word "within" in verse 33 is *bayith*, and it is defined as: house; court; inside ward (example: an enclosure, inside, or within). The word "without," in verse 35, in its Hebrew translation is *chuwts*, and it is defined as: to sever; separated by walls (example: outside or without). This further supports that the ark was specifically placed within the veil, in the Most Holy (Holy of Holies). The table and the candlestick were placed outside in the Holy Place (verse 35). These definitions are confirmed in several Jewish translations: *The Interlinear Bible* (Hebrew-English Concordance); *The Jerusalem Bible* (Jewish); and the *Complete Jewish Bible* (Jewish believers) to name just three.

Our God, who is not a God of confusion, was very specific as to the placement of the altar of incense as described in Exodus 30:6, "And you shall put it **before** the veil that *is* **before** the ark of the Testimony, **before** the mercy seat that *is* over the Testimony, where I will meet with you." In this verse we read that the altar of incense was to be placed before the veil, before the mercy seat. The word "before" used in the verse, is translated from the Hebrew word *paniym;* its primary definition is: before. Secondary translations include: presence; face; countenance; sight; forefront or forepart. When we look at the *American Heritage Dictionary* and other dictionaries as well, the word "before" is defined as: prior to; in front of. For instance, *BC* stands for, *time before Christ.* These translations of the word "before" substantiate the fact that the altar was positioned in front of the veil, before the mercy seat and not separated from the Holy of Holies by the veil. It was positioned in the presence of the Lord, before His face, in front of the mercy seat, where He would also meet with the priests. **See the illustration below.**

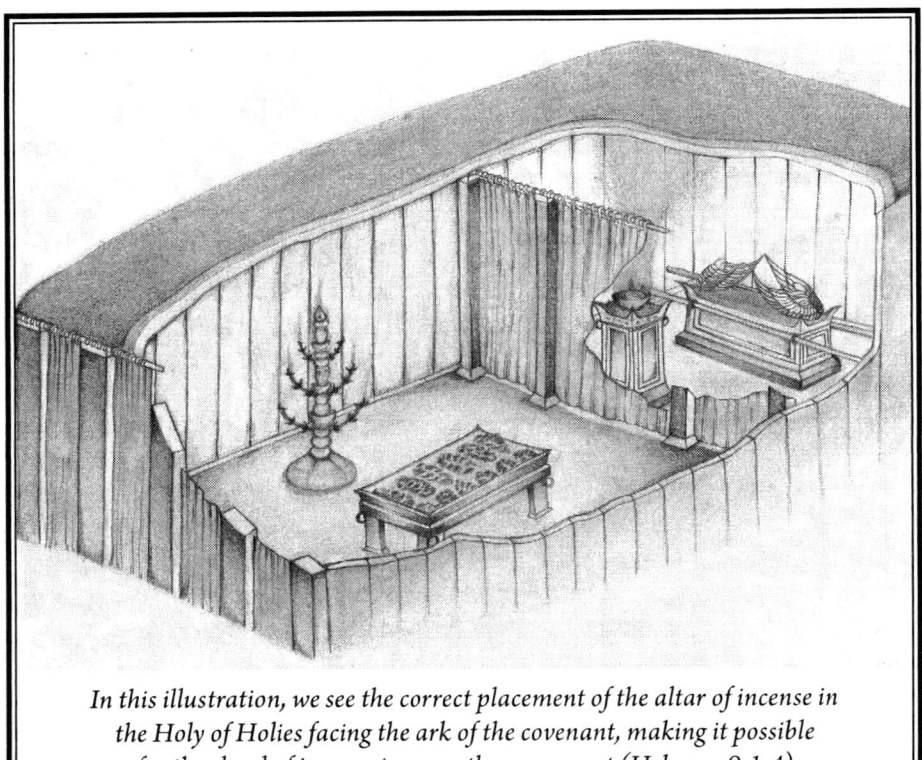

In this illustration, we see the correct placement of the altar of incense in the Holy of Holies facing the ark of the covenant, making it possible for the cloud of incense to cover the mercy seat (Hebrews 9:1-4).

For additional confirmation as to the placement of the articles of the tabernacle, we can look at the instructions given by the Lord to Moses, "And let them make Me a sanctuary, that I may dwell among them. "According to all that I show you, *that is*, the pattern of the tabernacle and the pattern of all its furnishings, just so you shall make *it*" (Exodus 25:8-9). Moses was instructed by the Lord to replicate the pattern that he was shown of the tabernacle in Heaven. The Lord wanted a physical place, an earthly sanctuary, where His people could direct their prayers and petitions. He gave His Word that He would hear their prayers and provide all of their needs.

When we look at Revelation 8:3 KJV, we can clearly see that the altar of incense was positioned before the throne. "And another angel came and stood at the altar, having a golden censer; and there was given unto him much incense, that he should offer *it* with the prayers of all saints upon **the golden altar which was before the throne**." The word "before" was translated from the Greek word *enopion,* and is defined as: in the face of; before; in the presence (sight) of. Therefore both the Hebrew word *paniym,* and the Greek word *enopion,* have the same meaning.

When we read about the building of the tabernacle and the arrangements of its furnishings the words "without" (*chuwts*), and "before" (*paniym*), are used to clarify the positioning of specific articles. "And he put the table in the tent of the congregation, upon the side of the tabernacle northward, **without** the veil. And he put the golden altar in the tent of the congregation **before** the veil" (Exodus 40:22,26 KJV).

The table of showbread and the lampstand were placed in the Holy Place, outside of the Holy of Holies. The golden altar (also referred to as the golden censer), upon which the incense was burned, was placed in the Holy of Holies; it was positioned before the veil, in the presence of the Lord. This again, as we saw earlier in this chapter, is also confirmed in Hebrews 9:1-4. In verse 2, it clearly states the following articles were placed in the sanctuary (the Holy Place): the lampstand, the table, and the showbread. In verses 3 and 4, we see that the golden censer and the ark of the covenant were located in the Holiest of All, more commonly known as the Holy of Holies.

> **Hebrews 9:2-4a** [2]For a tabernacle was prepared: the first *part*, in which *was* the lampstand, the table, and the showbread, which is called the sanctuary; [3]and behind the second veil, the part of the tabernacle which is called the Holiest of All, [4]which had the **golden censer** and the ark of the covenant overlaid on all sides with gold...

CHAPTER FOUR

THE ALTAR OF INCENSE IS SYMBOLIC OF OUR HEART

U nlike the arrangement of the other articles of the tabernacle which were clearly revealed by the Lord, we have discovered that we had to thoroughly examine the Word to determine the exact placement of the altar of incense. I shared earlier that this contributed to my difficulty in grasping that the altar of incense was, in fact, located in the Holy of Holies and not as I once believed, in the Holy Place. When I finally got out of my own way and allowed the Holy Spirit to guide me through the Word, I was able to receive the understanding clearly. I came to the realization that it was to my benefit that it took me so long to see the truth because it gave me more time to see the Lord's heart. The Lord brought me to the understanding that the altar of incense is symbolic of our hearts, just as the incense is symbolic of our praise. The heat of the burning coals represents the passion of our hearts; our passion fuels our desire to live our lives to please the Lord. It motivates us to sing praises unto Him, knowing that He is worthy of all our praise.

A grateful heart, one filled with passion fueling the desire to praise the Lord, likens itself to an altar of incense whose burning coals are hot enough to cause the incense to produce much smoke, creating clouds that ascend before the Lord. A heart that lacks passion, one that is unwilling to praise the Lord, likens itself to an altar whose coals are no longer burning, so they are not hot enough to produce clouds of smoke. The altar of incense is symbolic of our hearts and just as we had to thoroughly examine the Word to find its precise location, so must we thoroughly examine our lives to see where our hearts are in our relationship with the Lord.

Those of us that have come to understand the importance of praise and appreciate the opportunity to enter into the Holy of Holies must be careful not to present our praises in an indifferent, ritualistic manner. We must focus on God, who is the very reason for our praise. For when we do not, we will remain outside in the Holy Place. To enter into the presence of the Lord, into the Holy of Holies, we must first carefully check our hearts. We cannot allow our praises to be hindered by distractions caused by concerns or routines: thoughts of difficult situations, impending social events, or even just the mundane cares of our daily lives. When we do, we are allowing the enemy to rob the attention and the glory that belongs solely to God. Our praises should be presented from grateful hearts that are genuinely thankful for whom the Lord is and for all that He has done and continues to do for us.

It is an awesome privilege to present praise to the Lord; one we should not take lightly. We can only enter the Holy of Holies when we wholeheartedly understand that we serve a Lord who is worthy of all honor, all of the time. It is the brokenhearted, those with tears flowing down their faces, who in spite of their seemingly hopeless situations continue to willingly praise the Lord, who find themselves in the Holy of Holies. These are the ones who know that He is their only true hope. The Lord welcomes the tears of the brokenhearted, when they are shed in His midst, while seeking mercy, grace, and answers to prayers.

When we come to church, we are in the outer court. When we focus on singing heartfelt praises unto Him, we are clothing ourselves in the garments of praise which will take us into the presence of the Lord.

The Lord uses parables as a means to illustrate lessons concerning the issues of life. When we look at Luke, chapters 7 and 18, we will find biblical examples of individuals desperately seeking the Lord's tender mercy and taking hold of it.

> **Luke 7:44-48** Then He turned to the woman and said to Simon, "Do you see this woman? I entered your house; you gave Me no water for My feet, but she has washed My feet with her tears and wiped *them* with the hair of her head. "You gave Me no kiss, but this woman has not ceased to kiss My feet since the time I came in. "You did not anoint My head with oil, but this woman has anointed My feet with fragrant oil. "Therefore I say to you, her sins, *which are* many, are forgiven, for she loved much. But to whom little is forgiven, *the same* loves little." Then He said to her, "Your sins are forgiven."

Desperate to receive mercy from the Lord, the woman in this story arrives uninvited, at the home of a Pharisee, where she knew Jesus would be dining. Knowing that her morally offensive reputation preceded her, and in all likelihood the Pharisee would have had her thrown out, she boldly pressed in. Without uttering a single word, her actions touched the heart of the Lord and she received mercy and left forgiven.

> **Luke 18:10-14** "Two men went up to the temple to pray, one a Pharisee and the other a tax collector.

"The Pharisee stood and prayed thus with himself, 'God, I thank You that I am not like other men—extortioners, unjust, adulterers, or even as this tax collector. 'I fast twice a week; I give tithes of all that I possess.' "And the tax collector, standing afar off, would not so much as raise *his* eyes to heaven, but beat his breast, saying, 'God, be merciful to me a sinner!' "I tell you, this man went down to his house justified *rather* than the other; for everyone who exalts himself will be humbled, and he who humbles himself will be exalted."

The Lord uses this parable to demonstrate that it is not pleasing in His sight when we enter into His presence pridefully, exalting ourselves and judging others. God is not a respecter of persons; it is not our physical appearance, our possessions, our standing in society, our education, or our works that influence His willingness to extend His love or His mercy towards us. It is when we exalt Him above all things and in humility cry out to Him for mercy, for forgiveness of our sinful ways, that He is moved to justify us.

The Lord called David "a man after My own heart" (Acts 13:22); David knew how to take an unwavering hold of God's mercies. God extended this same mercy to Jesus, "And that He raised Him from the dead, no more to return to corruption, He has spoken thus: '*I will give you the sure mercies of David*' (Acts 13:34). God wants to extend this great mercy to all of us (Isaiah 53). We should learn to be like David. Despite having committed some gruesome sins, David continually praised God with a grateful heart; he did not allow his sins, to separate or to keep him separated from God, and so found grace for forgiveness and restoration. He knew that God was greater than anything his heart could use to condemn him. He understood that he served a God who was more than able and willing to deliver and restore him by His tender mercies. Here, once again, we can clearly see that there is a connection between praise and mercy; praise assists us in taking hold of God's mercies.

Psalm 51 should be the prayer of our hearts; we should continually be mindful and appreciative of what the Lord selflessly accomplished for us at the cross:

> **Psalm 51 Have mercy upon me, O God, According to Your lovingkindness; According to the multitude of Your tender mercies**, Blot out my transgressions. Wash me thoroughly from my iniquity, And cleanse me from my sin. For I acknowledge my transgressions, And my sin *is* always before me. Against You, You only, have I sinned, And done *this* evil in Your sight—That You may be found just when You speak, *And* blameless when You judge. Behold, I was brought forth in iniquity, And in sin my mother conceived me. Behold, You desire truth in the inward parts, And in the hidden *part* You will make me to know wisdom. Purge me with hyssop, and I shall be clean; Wash me, and I shall be whiter than snow. Make me hear joy and gladness, *That* the bones You have broken may rejoice. Hide Your face from my sins, And blot out all my iniquities. Create in me a clean heart, O God, And renew a steadfast spirit within me. Do not cast me away from Your presence, And do not take Your Holy Spirit from me. Restore to me the joy of Your salvation, And uphold me *by Your* generous Spirit. *Then* I will teach transgressors Your ways,

And sinners shall be converted to You. Deliver me from the quilt of bloodshed, O God, The God of my salvation, *And* my tongue shall sing aloud of Your righteousness. O Lord, open my lips, And my mouth shall show forth Your praise. For You do not desire sacrifice, or else I would give *it*; You do not delight in burnt offering. The sacrifices of God *are* a broken spirit, A broken and a contrite heart—These, O God, You will not despise. Do good in Your good pleasure to Zion; Build the walls of Jerusalem. Then You shall be pleased with the sacrifices of righteousness, With burnt offering and whole burnt offering; Then they shall offer bulls on Your altar.

Have you ever truly considered the magnitude of what was accomplished by Christ at the cross and to what extent we owe Him our very lives? Give the following some careful thought:

Imagine that you have become very sick and the doctor's prognosis is that without undergoing an immediate kidney transplant you will die. Someone willingly donates one of his kidneys; this person literally delivers you from a death sentence and you are given a second chance at life. You did nothing to deserve such a profound act of kindness. How thankful do you think you would be? Wouldn't this person who was responsible for saving your life be the person that proved their love for you the most? Wouldn't you boast to all you know about the depth of kindness this person bestowed upon you? Would it even be possible to measure your gratitude? Would this person who gave you the gift of life soon become the person you most love? Would this person be the guest of honor at the celebrations of life that mean the most to you? Now imagine that the very person responsible for saving your life becomes ill and dies as the result of health complications that his remaining kidney could not handle. You are standing at his burial sight, watching with deep sadness, as his body is lowered into the ground, knowing that his death was the result of his selfless act, he gave his life that you may live. How much more would your love for him deepen?

This hypothetical story represents only a shadow of what the Lord did for us, giving His life that we may live. How much more should we acknowledge that we could have no better friend than Jesus? Shouldn't we want to boast to all we know about what He did for us? Shouldn't He be the guest of honor at every celebration; isn't He the reason that we have things to celebrate? Jesus is responsible for every breath we take; shouldn't we want to love Him, praise Him, honor Him, and glorify His name?

Although the above story is fictitious, in the field of medicine, there are countless documented cases in which selfless acts of giving blood, organs, bone marrow, even one's life (when a mother dies during childbirth) that are responsible for one person giving of their own life to save another's. There are also similar accounts in the military; those that serve in the armed forces, especially in times of war, risk life and limb not only for the nations they defend, but for their fellow servicemen as well. One such account was depicted in the motion picture, *Saving Private Ryan*.

The film's story was inspired by the real-life Niland brothers who served in the military during World War II. The plot of the movie is centered around a World War II private, James Ryan, who is missing in action during the Normandy Invasion. It details the courageous acts of seven rangers who were ordered to find him. Their assignment was an act of mercy on behalf of Ryan's mother, who unbeknownst to her, was soon to receive word that her other three sons (also on active duty) were killed in action. Their mission was to find Ryan so he could immediately be sent home, in hopes that the life of a mother's only remaining son might be spared. The film opens in France, where an elderly World War II veteran, James Ryan, along with his wife and family, are visiting the Normandy American Cemetery and Memorial. Overwhelmed with emotion, Ryan falls to his knees in the midst of countless grave markers. The scene fades out and reopens many years earlier with the beginning of the Normandy Invasion. The film concludes in the present, as Ryan kneels in front of the burial site of the fallen captain, who along with four of his men lost their lives, so his could be spared. He recalls the captain's dying words to him; *James…earn this. Earn it.* He speaks softly, addressing the gravesite of the captain, saying that he tried his hardest to live every day the best he could. Looking for validation, Ryan turns to his wife and asks; *Did I earn it? Am I a good man? Did I live a good life? Am I worthy of the grave price that was paid for it?*

How much more should we purpose in our hearts to live our lives worthy of the supreme sacrifice the Lord made for our sakes, when He willingly gave His life, so we may live? Shouldn't we want to continually live our lives in a manner that properly honors Him, for all He did for us, and for all He continues to do? Is He not worthy of hearts that are full of passion fueled with a burning desire to, above all things, praise Him?

Romans 5:6-8 For when we were still without strength, in due time Christ died for the ungodly. For scarcely for a righteous man will one die; yet perhaps for a good man someone would even dare to die. But God demonstrates His own love toward us, in that while we were still sinners, Christ died for us.

Giving of one's life, not knowing if the act of sacrifice will be detrimental to one's own survival is true heroism; it is a true act of selfless courage. But how much more courageous is an act of heroism that you know beforehand, will ultimately result in your death. Jesus was not ordered to the cross; He went willingly. He yielded Himself for our sakes. He gave His life willingly to show His love for us. He gave it so we could have life and life more abundantly (John 10:10).

We all want to one day stand before the Lord and know that we lived our lives worthy of the sacrifice of His life.

CHAPTER FIVE

COME BOLDLY

Let us therefore come boldly to the throne of grace, that we may
obtain mercy and find grace to help in time of need.
Hebrews 4:16

The word "boldly," in the above Scripture, is translated from
the Greek word *parrhesia;* its English translation is: confidently. It is used to describe the manner of one's speech:
"come boldly to the throne of grace" (come confidently declaring
God's goodness and His tender mercies). Speak (pray) plainly,
frankly, with surety, knowing your prayers are being heard, declare that whatever provision (forgiveness, healing, deliverance,
restoration, etc.) you are seeking from God, will be faithfully provided (1 John 5:14-15).

Many times when we are faced with a difficult situation, and
it is necessary for us to pray, we try to stir up our faith, but faith
is not an emotional state of belief. Faith is a fact; it believes in
the unchanging Word of God. When we base our assurance in
God on our emotions, or on how we feel at any given moment,
we are opening the door for the enemy to bring doubts and fears

that God is not hearing our prayers. When our faith (confidence, trust, assurance) in God remains constant (unwavering) we are always prepared to do battle with the enemy and we will always be victorious.

In the past the most outspoken men, those who were extremely forthright and bold in speech, would become the leaders of the church, the evangelists, etc. Miracles were performed as they effortlessly declared God's Word; they spoke openly, plainly, and boldly, sharing God's benefits (His goodness, His promises) with the people. They were doing exactly what the Lord wants all of us to do. We all have the same faith; their faith was not greater than ours. It was their boldness and their outspokenness that glorified the Lord and brought miracles. We do not need to be preachers to do the same. If we simply declare with our lips the goodness of God, regardless of the thoughts (doubts, fears) our minds may be bombarded with, we too will witness miracles in our lives.

Do not be intimidated by the wrongs you have committed; do not allow your heart to condemn you with feelings of unworthiness; do not speak (pray) words of fear or doubt (1 John 3:18-22). When we question whether our prayers are God's will, or use the words *if* or *but* when we pray, we are showing a lack of faith. Come boldly with the authority you have been given in the name of Jesus to ask and to know the answer to your prayer is not based on your righteousness, but on the unchanging Word (promises) and mercy of God. This is what the Holy Spirit was referring to through the prophet Isaiah, in Isaiah 1:18, "Come now, and let us reason together." The word "reason" means: to talk things out, logically and persuasively. He is not forcing anyone to do or to ask anything. He is inviting us into His presence, "come." He is asking us not to hesitate, "come now." He is encouraging us, "let us reason together," let us talk. The Lord goes on to say if you come, though your sins may be as "scarlet" (terrible), you will be forgiven and you will enjoy the benefits of the land.

Years ago, during my prison outreach ministry, I shared this very message based on the promises of God written in Isaiah 1:18. I told the men that Jesus paid the price for their sins on the cross, but that society also requires that they (the inmates) pay a price for the crimes they committed. One of the inmates took hold of what he heard that day and boldly prayed, asking the Lord, that if He (Jesus) truly paid the price for his sins (the reasons that he was incarcerated) could He, at this time grant him favor; he asked the Lord to be released from prison. Two days later, many months ahead of schedule, he was called before the parole board. He was released from prison the following week. He violently (boldly) took hold of the Lord's mercy and found freedom.

David came to understand this and so possessed an unwavering confidence in the mercy of God. While others, fearing death, would not dare enter the Holy of Holies, the presence of the ark of the covenant, David entered at will. His faith, in the reality of God's mercies, gave him the boldness to enter in whenever he had a need to speak to the Lord. He would not only walk out alive, but he would walk out forgiven and blessed with the answer he sought. David did not allow his own weaknesses to hinder him, or prevent him from entering God's presence for the purpose of offering praises, or lifting prayers before Him. David's faith enabled him to trust in God's mercy. He believed without hesitation that his prayers would be answered. David's continual praise of the Lord acted as a cloud of incense covering the mercy seat, allowing him to enter the presence of God, without fear, whenever he had a need.

Many people do not truly realize that God wants them to enter His presence boldly, giving thanks and lifting praises (incense). It is true, grace covers a multitude of situations but the Word warns us, "let us not do wrong that grace may abound." The sacrifice of praise is what the Lord requires of us today; it is the awesome power in obtaining mercy and finding grace. Petitions should not be lifted before praises (thanksgiving) are presented to God. Consider the following song lyrics by Kirk Dearman:

> *We bring the sacrifice of praise into the house of the Lord.*
> *We bring the sacrifice of praise into the house of the Lord.*
> *And we offer up to You the sacrifices of thanksgiving. And*
> *we offer up to You the sacrifices of praise.*

Offering up the sacrifice of praise, continually before the Lord, predates the Book of Hebrews; we see it written in Exodus, with the building and function instructions of the altar of incense. Today, we can do as David did; we can come boldly into God's presence whenever we have a need. There is no longer a veil that impedes us from entering God's presence. The sacrifice of Christ Jesus on the cross has removed all obstacles. We should not only enter the presence of the Lord when we have a need, we should also enter to worship Him, above and before all things. He is worthy of all of our praise. "Therefore by Him let us continually offer the sacrifice of praise to God, that is, the fruit of *our* lips, giving thanks to His name" (Hebrews 13:15).

Christ's sacrifice made it possible for us to enter into God's presence at will, unlike the priests who before the cross, had to fulfill specific requirements to have the same privilege. It was essential that the priests be in the right frame of mind before entering into God's presence. The gold plate and turban described in the verses to follow represent the proper attitude required of the priest:

> **Exodus 28:36-38** "You shall also make a plate of pure gold and engrave on it, *like* the engraving of a signet: HOLINESS TO THE LORD. "And you shall put it

on a blue cord, that it may be on the turban; it shall be on the front of the turban. "So it shall be on Aaron's forehead, that Aaron may bear the iniquity of the holy things which the children of Israel hallow in all their holy gifts; and it shall always be on his forehead, **that they may be accepted before the LORD.**

What gave the high priest entry to the Holy of Holies prior to him burning the incense? In the following we will clearly see, by the provision God made, His great desire for us to come and enter His presence. God Himself provided the way. We know that it was the smoke of the burning incense that kept the high priest alive while He was in the presence of God (Leviticus 16:12-13); now, let us look at what the mercy of God provided to grant the high priest admittance to the Holy of Holies *before* the incense was burned.

God commanded that a robe be created, according to His specific instructions; it was the wearing of this garment that allowed the high priest safe access into the Holy of Holies. The robe was designed by God to be an instrument of praise. It was adorned with bells of gold attached to its hem. The *musical* sounds the bells produced as the high priest walked into the Holy of Holies kept him alive; thus, allowing him to approach the altar of incense. There, he would burn the incense necessary to cover the mercy seat with the cloud, enabling him to continue with the daily process of presenting the needs/prayers of the people and once a year the blood offering before God.

> **Exodus 28:31,33-35** "You shall make the robe of the ephod all of blue. "And upon its hem you shall make pomegranates of blue, purple, and scarlet, all around its hem, and **bells of gold** between them all around: "a golden bell and a pomegranate, a golden bell and a

pomegranate, upon the hem of the robe all around. "And it shall be upon Aaron when he ministers, and its sound will be heard when he goes into the holy *place* before the LORD and when he comes out, **that he may not die**."

Those who have not yet come to understand the significance of the bells on the hem of the priest's robe, commonly believe that the priest would enter the tabernacle with a rope tied around his ankle. If the priest did not come out of the tabernacle, those on the outside, perceiving he had died and fearing for their own safety could, without entering the Holy Place, pull him out by the rope. The origin of this *belief* can be traced back to what happened to the sons of Aaron, when they entered the presence of God and died. Many of these misconceptions instill a fear of approaching God, while He (the Lord), asks us to come no matter what we have done.

In Exodus 28:33-35 we saw, clearly revealed, the significance of the bells on the hem of the high priest's robe. But what was the significance of the pomegranates? I asked the Lord that very question on my return flight home from Africa, after my first international demonstration of the *Incense Is Symbolic of Praise* presentation (see chapter 22). The Lord shared that the pomegranate represented the collective prayers of the saints enveloped in praise. I was overwhelmed by His response; the answer was always there. The pomegranate has hundreds of seeds, each encased in its own fruit, each with its own membrane-type skin. There are hundreds of them, representing the prayers of the saints. Each is a fruit, independent of the others; each is symbolic of its own prayer (seed) enveloped in praise (fruit). It is wonderful to realize that our Lord created a fruit, representative of our prayers, which deals with the faith of our hearts. Additionally, the pomegranate is also an antioxidant that helps to keep our hearts healthy.

The Lord instructed that pomegranates, which represented the combined prayers of the saints, and golden bells (praise) be attached in an alternating sequence to the hem of the robe, which was required to be worn by the high priest before he could enter the Holy Place. Here again, we can see that just as our prayers should be enveloped (surrounded) by praise, the pomegranates

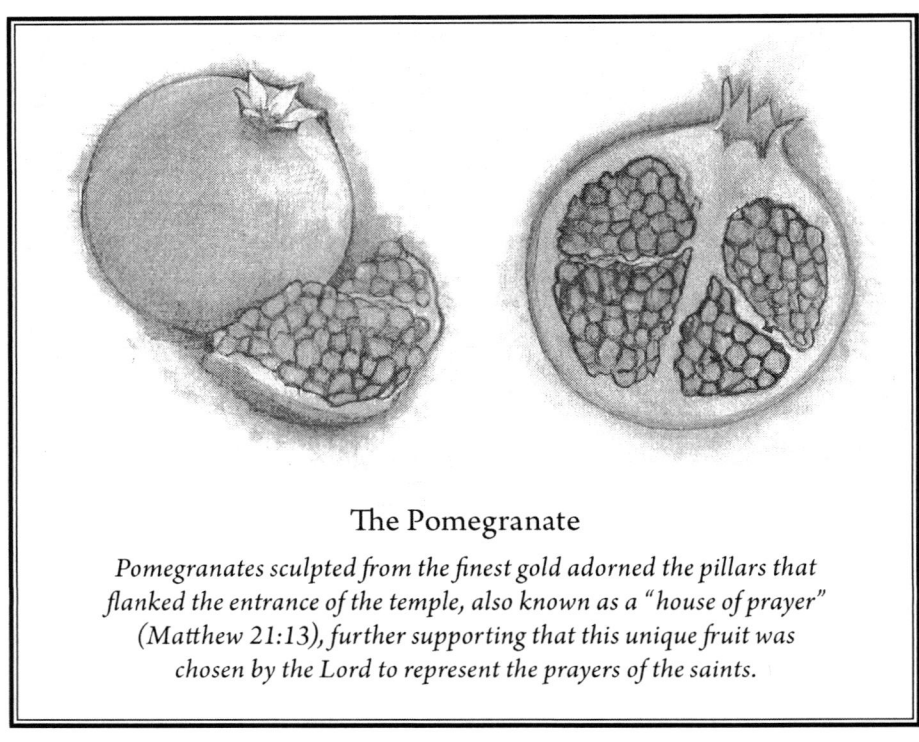

The Pomegranate

Pomegranates sculpted from the finest gold adorned the pillars that flanked the entrance of the temple, also known as a "house of prayer" (Matthew 21:13), further supporting that this unique fruit was chosen by the Lord to represent the prayers of the saints.

were surrounded by symbolic bells of praise. After entering the tabernacle with the right attitude, wearing the appropriate garments, the priests would then offer up incense (the precursor to praise) before the Lord. By fulfilling these requirements, the priest was kept alive:

> **Leviticus 16:12-13** "Then he shall take a censer full of burning coals of fire from the altar before the LORD,

with his hands full of sweet incense beaten fine, and bring *it* inside the veil. "And he shall put the incense on the fire before the LORD, that the cloud of incense may cover the mercy seat that *is* on the Testimony, **lest he die.**

The Lord required a pure desire to praise Him, for who He was, for what He had provided, and for what He would continue to provide, before any petitions were lifted. Only after the offering of incense (praise) covered the mercy seat was the priest permitted to offer the blood of a sacrificial bull before the Lord as atonement for sin.

Leviticus 16:14 "He shall take some of the blood of the bull and sprinkle *it* with his finger on the mercy seat on the east *side;* and before the mercy seat he shall sprinkle some of the blood with his finger seven times.

As we read earlier, Exodus 30:7-10 reveals that incense was always present, even before the offering of blood. The Lord required that incense be burned twice a day, every day. The blood offering was brought by the high priest into the Holy of Holies only once a year, on the Day of Atonement (Yom Kippur), it was sprinkled before the ark of the covenant and applied to the horns of the altar of incense after the incense was burning. Just as the priests were required to bring the incense (praise) before the Lord prior to bringing the blood (atonement), we are asked to do the same. We should first exalt the Lord with the praises of our lips and with the right attitude, being mindful that we are entering the presence of an awesome, loving, merciful Father. We should pray like the example (manner) the Lord sets before us in Matthew 6:9-13,

"In this manner, therefore, pray: Our Father in heaven, Hallowed be Your name. Your kingdom come. Your will be done On earth as *it is* in heaven. Give us this day our daily bread. And forgive us our debts, As we forgive our debtors. And do not lead us into temptation, But deliver us from the evil one. For Yours is the kingdom and the power and the glory forever. Amen."

The Lord Himself taught us to pray in the manner that would most please the Father. He instructed us to first offer up our praises, declaring His greatness, by worshiping Him, acknowledging all that He means to us: He is our Savior; our Deliverer; our Healer; our Provider; and our Peace. We should also remind ourselves of testimonies of His goodness towards us, and we should willingly offer before Him heartfelt songs of praise. We should do these things before asking Him for forgiveness, deliverance, healing, restoration, etc. We can freely enter into His presence as we clothe ourselves in garments of praise. This is accomplished when we focus on the words we present in praise, and from the very depths of our hearts, we praise the Lord for whom He is.

CHAPTER SIX

DO NOT COME PRESUMPTUOUSLY

The high priest was kept alive by entering and leaving God's presence with a praise offering. The Lord warned the priest not to enter His presence with an attitude of indifference. Aaron's two sons did not obey the Lord's warning. Neither was chosen/anointed by the Lord to be a high priest, so they were not attired in the garments that the high priest alone was consecrated to wear. The priests that served under the high priest had their own garments as described in Exodus 29:5-6, 8-9. They were not protected by the robe with the bells of gold (instruments of praise) as described in Exodus 28, which sounds gave safe access to the Holy of Holies, the presence of God.

The Lord did not choose/anoint Aaron's sons to burn incense before Him, "each took his censer and put fire in it, put incense on it, and offered profane fire before the LORD, which He had not commanded them" (Leviticus 10:1b). The word "profane" used in the verse, signifies that the offering of incense was presented contemptuously, presumptuously, with irreverence before a Holy God. The word "profane," in its Hebrew translation is *zuwr*, and it is defined as: a foreigner, stranger, profane.

It is also used to refer to the advances of a strange woman, or to someone committing adultery. Aaron's sons paid the price for their willful disobedience with their lives. "So fire went out from the LORD and devoured them, and they died before the LORD" (Leviticus 10:2).

The high priest would clothe himself in his priestly garments, with the bells of gold, before presenting the burning incense in the presence of the Lord. We should look upon the priest's preparation as a representation of readying ourselves (preparing our hearts) to go before the Lord to present our praises. We should acknowledge that we are entering the presence of an awesome, holy, merciful, and loving Father with whom nothing is impossible. The Lord provided the way, then and now, for us to freely come, " 'By those who come near Me I must be regarded as holy; And before all the people I must be glorified' " (Leviticus 10:3b). The "veil," which was symbolic of the sins of our flesh that once separated us from the Holy of Holies (God's presence), was forever taken away. We can now, without any hindrance, praise our way into the presence of God, "by a new and living way which He consecrated for us, through the veil, that is, His flesh" (Hebrews 10:20).

When we read on we can see the way that God provided for Aaron, the high priest, to enter into His presence:

> **Leviticus 16:2-14** …and the LORD said to Moses: "Tell Aaron your brother not to come at *just* any time into the Holy *Place* inside the veil, before the mercy seat which *is* on the ark, lest he die; for I will appear in the cloud above the mercy seat. "Thus Aaron shall come into the Holy *Place:* with *the blood of* a young bull as a sin offering, and *of* a ram as a burnt offering. "He shall put the holy linen tunic and the linen trousers on his body; he shall

be girded with a linen sash, and with the linen turban he shall be attired. These *are* holy garments. Therefore he shall wash his body in water, and put them on. "And he shall take from the congregation of the children of Israel two kids of the goats as a sin offering, and one ram as a burnt offering. "Aaron shall offer the bull as a sin offering, which *is* for himself, and make atonement for himself and for his house. "He shall take the two goats and present them before the LORD *at* the door of the tabernacle of meeting. "Then Aaron shall cast lots for the two goats: one lot for the LORD and the other lot for the scapegoat. "And Aaron shall bring the goat on which the LORD's lot fell, and offer it *as* a sin offering. "But the goat on which the lot fell to be the scapegoat shall be presented alive before the LORD, to make atonement upon it, *and* to let it go as the scapegoat into the wilderness. "And Aaron shall bring the bull of the sin offering, which is for himself, and make atonement for himself and for his house, and shall kill the bull as a sin offering which *is* for himself. "Then he shall take a censer full of burning coals of fire from the altar before the LORD, with his hands full of sweet incense beaten fine, and bring *it* inside the veil. "And he shall put the incense on the fire before the LORD, that the cloud of incense may cover the mercy seat that *is* on the Testimony, lest he die. "He shall take some of the blood of the bull and sprinkle *it* with his finger on the mercy seat on the east *side;* and before the mercy seat he shall sprinkle some of the blood with his finger seven times.

To summarize Leviticus 16:2-14, the key components necessary to enter into God's presence for the purpose of forgiveness of sins were:

- the right attitude—which represents the condition of our heart; a broken and contrite heart, a humble heart (humility)

Psalm 51:17 The sacrifices of God *are* a broken spirit, A broken and a contrite heart—These, O God, You will not despise.

Isaiah 57:15 For thus says the High and Lofty One Who inhabits eternity, whose name *is* Holy: "I dwell in the high and holy *place*, With him *who* has a contrite and humble spirit, To revive the spirit of the humble, And to revive the heart of the contrite ones.

- incense and the bells of gold—which today are represented by the praise of our lips
- blood (the pouring out of blood)—which was and still is required for the atonement, forgiveness of sins

Jesus Himself fulfilled these requirements while on the earth: He sang hymns (praise) with His disciples after breaking bread with them (Matthew 26:30); He prayed to His Father (Matthew 26:39); and He shed blood for the forgiveness of our sins (Matthew 27:35).

Not only was atonement for man's sins made once a year by blood, on and before the mercy seat, it was also made on the horns of the altar of incense (Exodus 30:10). Thus, we clearly see that praise not only preceded, but it also prepared the way for the blood.

> **Exodus 30:10** "And Aaron shall make atonement upon its horns once a year with the blood of the sin offering of atonement; once a year he shall make atonement upon it throughout your generations. It *is* most holy to the LORD."

CHAPTER SEVEN

LET NOTHING STOP YOU

David boldly entered God's presence regardless of his sins. He did not allow his heart (feelings of guilt or unworthiness) to condemn him or stop him. David had confidently come to know that God's mercy was greater than any sin that his heart could use to condemn him. God wants us all to have that same confidence. The Word revealed to David that the Lord wants to justify His people, no matter what they have done. All that is required of us is to forsake (renounce, abandon) our wrong ways of life; turn to Him; repent; and wholeheartedly cry out for forgiveness. He promises to hear us, to forgive us, and to restore us.

> **Isaiah 1:18** "Come now, and let us reason together," Says the LORD, "Though your sins are like scarlet, They shall be as white as snow; Though they are red like crimson, They shall be as wool.

> **Isaiah 55:6-7** Seek the LORD while He may be found, Call upon Him while He is near. Let the wicked forsake his way, And the unrighteous man

his thoughts; Let him return to the LORD, And He will have mercy on him; And to our God, For He will abundantly pardon.

David's primary motivation for praising God was to thank Him for His endless mercies and His loving kindness. It is written, "For if our heart condemns us, God is greater than our heart, and knows all things" (1 John 3:20). This is true; we must possess a fear of God because whom we fear we will obey. And the fear of reaping the consequences of our wrongdoings, or the fear of displeasing God and finding ourselves outside of His will, is what deters us from succumbing to sin.

However, when our stubborn or rebellious natures cause us to commit sin, we must not allow the enemy to instill fear in us. Fears of unworthiness hinder us from entering God's presence. Regardless of our wrongdoings, God is always worthy of praise. We should continually thank Him for His mercies, for dying for our sins. We empower the enemy when we allow him to manipulate our thoughts, convincing us that we can no longer enter into God's presence. Just as David did before us, God wants us to come boldly into His presence, to first praise Him for whom He is, and then to ask Him to forgive us our transgressions. He is a great and merciful Father who knows our frailties and is faithful to forgive us and to restore us.

People often make it difficult for the backslidden, placing too many requirements on them before they are permitted to return back into the fellowship of the church. The prodigal son did not suffer any of those experiences; he was welcomed back into the loving arms of his father. He was received with honors and a grand homecoming feast despite his brother's objections.

Luke 15:11-32 Then He said: "A certain man had two sons. "And the younger of them said to *his* father, 'Father, give me the portion of goods that falls *to me.*' So he divided to them *his* livelihood. "And not many days after, the younger son gathered all together, journeyed to a far country, and there wasted his possessions with prodigal living. "But when he had spent all, there arose a severe famine in that land, and he began to be in want. "Then he went and joined himself to a citizen of that country, and he sent him into his fields to feed swine. "And he would gladly have filled his stomach with the pods that the swine ate, and no one gave him *anything.* "But when he came to himself, he said, 'How many of my father's hired servants have bread enough and to spare, and I perish with hunger! 'I will arise and go to my father, and will say to him, "Father, I have sinned against heaven and before you, and I am no longer worthy to be called your son. Make me like one of your hired servants." ' "And he arose and came to his father. But when he was still a great way off, his father saw him and had compassion, and ran and fell on his neck and kissed him. "And the son said to him, 'Father, I have sinned against heaven and in your sight, and am no longer worthy to be called your son.' "But the father said to his servants, 'Bring out the best robe and put *it* on him, and put a ring on his hand and sandals on *his* feet. 'And bring the fatted calf here and kill *it,* and let us eat and be merry; 'for this my son was dead and is alive again; he was lost and is found.' And they began to be merry. "Now his older son was in the field. And as he came and drew near to the house, he heard music and dancing. "So he called one of the servants and asked what these things meant. "And he said to him, 'Your brother has come, and because he has received him safe and sound, your father has killed the fatted calf.' "But he was angry and would not go in. Therefore his father came out and pleaded with him. "So he answered and said to *his* father, 'Lo, these many years I have been serving you; I never transgressed your commandment at any time; and yet you never gave me a young goat, that I might make merry with my friends. 'But as soon as this son of yours came, who has devoured your livelihood with harlots, you killed the fatted calf for him.' "And he said to him, 'Son, you are always with me, and all that I have is yours. 'It was right that we should make merry and be glad, for your brother was dead and is alive again, and was lost and is found.'"

The *Parable of the Prodigal Son* is a simple story with an important message. The father in the story is a representation of our Heavenly Father; he is loving, merciful, and forgiving. And just as our Father in Heaven does not impose His will on us, the father in the story allows his son to make his own choices. The results of the son's poor decisions put him on a path of destruction, a path whose course, if left unchanged, would lead to death. By the grace of God, the prodigal son comes to realize that he was grossly mistaken in leaving his father's home and decides to return. "I will arise and go to my father, and will say to him, "Father, I have sinned against heaven and before you, and I am no longer worthy to be called your son. Make me like one of your hired servants" (Luke 15:18-19).

His father, overwhelmed with joy and compassion at the sight of his returning son, without hesitation lovingly welcomes him back into his heart and into his home. Our Heavenly Father does the same for us when we choose the path of a backslider and then ask for forgiveness; He welcomes us back into His heart and He embraces us with His love. We should all follow the example the Lord has set before us in this parable. We should never judge as the brother in the story, or compare our righteousness with the righteousness of another. "He who is without sin among you, let him throw a stone at her first" (John 8:7b). God is not a respecter of persons; it is His great desire not to see any souls go lost. He has set before us the perfect example, Jesus, through whom we should all learn to forgive unconditionally.

The following is the true story about a backslider's return to church and to the Lord. For the sake of his privacy, let us refer to him as Paul.

Two weeks before Paul was to marry the woman he loved, she left him for another man. Devastated and heartbroken, and not realizing like so many of us, that when trials come the best place for us to be is in the presence of the Lord, he stopped going to church. Sometime later he met and fell in love with another woman. His fear of history repeating itself kept him from asking her to marry him. The two moved in together without the benefit of marriage. One day, someone encouraged them to attend a Sunday service at our church. They came, and at the close of service, they both accepted Christ into their hearts; Paul recommitted his life to the Lord and his girlfriend committed hers for the first time. They began to attend church faithfully. As their living arrangements became more openly known, church members began sharing their objections about their lifestyle. Even Paul's mother voiced her objections about her son and his live-in girlfriend being welcomed, by me (the pastor), into the house of the Lord. The situation worsened when Paul's girlfriend became pregnant. They continued to come to church and they were finally married when their son was a toddler. When they returned from their honeymoon, a tearful Paul thanked me for not giving up on him; he thanked me for patiently counseling him and for helping him to be healed from his painful past experiences, enabling him to conquer his fear of rejection. He gratefully declared, "Thank you, Pastor, for being patient with me, if it had been another church, I might have been put out."

Only God knows if Paul would have remained a backslider and unmarried if he had been asked to leave the church. It is not for us to judge, we must learn to justify one another and to show the love and the patience for others that we ourselves want to receive.

CHAPTER EIGHT

PRAISE IS NOT A COVER FOR WRONG

Praise takes us into the presence of God; it prepares the way for us to approach our merciful Father to ask His forgiveness for the wrongs we have committed. Wrongs are not always willfully committed, but regardless of whether or not we knowingly commit an act that is contrary to the Word of God, there will always be consequences. The only way for us to avoid the consequences of sin is for us to learn how to guard ourselves against committing it. The best way to do that is to arm ourselves with "the sword of the Spirit, which is the word of God" (Ephesians 6:17b). We can only defend ourselves with the Word when we make the decision to learn it and live by it.

God knows the battles that lie ahead of us; He wants to prepare us for them so that we will come through them victoriously. He prepares us in church, by the Holy Spirit, through our pastors. It is the degree of our faithfulness (our attendance in church), as we consciously listen to what the Holy Spirit has to say through our pastors, that will determine our preparedness to do battle with the enemy. "My people are destroyed for lack of knowledge" (Hosea 4:6).

Luke 12:47-48 "And that servant who knew his master's will, and did not prepare *himself* or do according to his will, shall be beaten with many *stripes.* "But he who did not know, yet committed things deserving of stripes, shall be beaten with few. For everyone to whom much is given, from him much will be required; and to whom much has been committed, of him they will ask the more.

Both servants in the Scriptures were deservedly held accountable. However, the servant who knew the will of his master and chose to deliberately disobey him was punished more severely than the servant who was ignorant (unaware) of his master's will.

Praise does not have the power, on its own, to excuse or absolve our transgressions; that power comes as praise helps us to take hold of the tender mercies and loving kindness of God. Consider the following as an example of one of those occasions:

Luke 7:44-48 Then He turned to the woman and said to Simon, "Do you see this woman? I entered your house; you gave Me no water for My feet, but she has washed My feet with her tears and wiped *them* with the hair of her head. "You gave Me no kiss, but this woman has not ceased to kiss My feet since the time I came in. "You did not anoint My head with oil, but this woman has anointed My feet with fragrant oil. "Therefore I say to you, her sins, *which are* many, are forgiven, for she loved much. But to whom little is forgiven, *the same* loves little." Then He said to her, "Your sins are forgiven."

Praise takes hold of God's mercies as we show the brokenness of our hearts and our love for the Lord. Praise is not always vocalized (actions speak louder than words); it can sometimes be shown by the physical expression of love and admiration. It was not necessary for the woman to utter a single word; it was the sincerity of her actions, her display of contriteness as she washed the Lord's feet with her heartfelt tears, dried them with the hair of her head, kissed them, and anointed them with oil, that moved on the heart of the Lord to forgive her.

Let us look at some biblical examples of times when praise alone was not enough to cover or excuse the wrongdoer when he had the opportunity to know the truth. In 2 Samuel 6, we can read about David's failed attempt to transport the ark of the Lord from Beth Shemesh to the City of David (Jerusalem), when he allowed it to be transported on a cart drawn by oxen. David did not wait on the Lord for proper instructions. Instead, he allowed himself to be influenced by the religious ignorance of the Philistines (1 Samuel 6); the consequences for his decision brought death. The Lord required that the ark be carried on the shoulders of sanctified Levite priests, not pulled by oxen on a cart. The praises that David and his leaders offered the Lord did not acquit them while they were doing their wrong. Praise is not a cover for *ignorance*. In the same way that ignorance did not excuse David's erroneous acts, it will not excuse ours. "Truly, these times of ignorance God overlooked, but now commands all men everywhere to repent" (Acts 17:30).

The Lord wants to reveal His Word,
and the understanding of it, to all that seek it.

After seeing that doing things his own way brought severe consequences, David sought the Lord's instructions as to the proper way to transport the ark. When we choose to do things according to God's instructions (His Word), He helps us because He is faithful to watch over His Word to perform it.

> **1 Chronicles 15:2, 11-15** Then David said, "**No one may carry the ark of God but the Levites, for the LORD has chosen them to carry the ark of God and to minister before Him forever.**" And David called for Zadok and Abiathar the priests, and for the Levites: for Uriel, Asaiah, Joel, Shemaiah, Eliel, and Amminadab. He said to them, "You *are* the heads of the fathers' *houses* of the Levites; sanctify yourselves, you and your brethren, that you may bring up the ark of the LORD God of Israel to *the place* I have prepared for it. "**For because you *did* not *do it* the first *time*, the LORD our God broke out against us, because we did not consult Him about the proper order.**" So the priests and the Levites sanctified themselves to bring up the ark of the LORD God of Israel. And the children of the Levites bore the ark of God on their shoulders, by its poles, as Moses had commanded according to the word of the LORD.

Another example found in the Word concerning praise *not* being a covering for disobedience can be found when we read 2 Samuel, chapters 11 and 12. These chapters detail the events that took place when David coveted Bathsheba, another man's wife, to the extent of purposefully sending him to his death. The price for David's sin was paid for with the death of the child his union with Bathsheba produced.

When we read 2 Samuel 24, we will find yet another example of a grave price being the wage for disobeying God's Word. It details a time when David ordered that the people of Israel and Judah be numbered. Seventy thousand men died as the result of a plague that David's disobedience brought about; his life of praise did not cover him in his wrongs. Praise covers us as we set out to do what is right with a right (sanctified) heart, separating ourselves from the wrong we do. When we praise with a right heart, exalting God's greatness and His mercies, we are able to enter into His presence. That is when we obtain our covering and when we receive answers to our petitions.

> **2 Samuel 22:49-51** He delivers me from my enemies. You also lift me up above those who rise against me; You have delivered me from the violent man. Therefore I will give thanks to You, O LORD, among the Gentiles, And sing praises to Your name. *He is* the tower of salvation to His king, And shows mercy to His anointed, To David and his descendants forevermore."

For many years scholars have wondered what allowed David to enter the Holy of Holies, and to stand before the mercy seat, in the presence of God. He was not a priest, he did not wear the required robe adorned with bells, nor did he burn incense prior to entering. David's life of continual praise was a live representation of the incense and the bells. It was that praise that covered his entrance into God's presence; it gave him favor with God. "So then *it is* not of him who wills, nor of him who runs, but of God who shows mercy" (Romans 9:16).

None of us are deserving of God's goodness but
nevertheless it is God, who in His great mercy, watches over us.

CHAPTER NINE

PRAISE IS ORDAINED FOR THE SERVICES

We have learned in earlier chapters that incense was burned twice a day and the cloud of smoke that was produced was symbolic of the praise that was required by the Lord before entering His presence. We have also learned that a specially constructed robe, adorned with bells, was worn by the high priest. The musical sounds, the bells made as the priest walked about, permitted him safe access into the Holy of Holies, where he would burn incense on the altar, meet with the Lord, and present to Him the petitions of the people.

Because David came to understand the importance of praising the Lord for His endless mercy, God placed it on David's heart to institute the live praise and worship He desired for the services. David created various musical instruments and he appointed musicians and singers to praise the Lord, twice daily, in the morning and again in the evening, and at every burnt offering.

1 Chronicles 23:5b …four thousand praised the
LORD with *musical* instruments, "which I made,"
said David, "for giving praise."

1 Chronicles 23:30-31 …stand every morning to
thank and praise the LORD, and likewise at evening;
and at every presentation of a burnt offering to the
LORD…

2 Chronicles 7:6 And the priests attended to their
services; the Levites also with instruments of the
music of the LORD, which King David had made
to praise the LORD, saying, "For His mercy *endures*
forever," whenever David offered praise by their
ministry. The priests sounded trumpets opposite
them, while all Israel stood.

Live praise and worship was first introduced during the services (sacrificial ceremonies) when the ark of the Lord was brought to the tabernacle that David had erected. David not only ordained praise and worship, he was deeply involved as well.

1 Chronicles 16:1,4 KJV So they brought the ark of
God, and set it in the midst of the tent that David
had pitched for it.…And he appointed *certain* of the
Levites to minister before the ark of the LORD, and
to record, and to thank and praise the LORD God
of Israel…

The word "record" is translated from the Hebrew word *zakar;* it is defined as: to bring back to memory, by implication; to make mention (example: petition, prayer). In His Word, God asks

His people to remind Him of His promises. The Levites were appointed to minister in prayer, and to give thanks and praise to the Lord.

When we look at 2 Chronicles 8:14-15, we will find confirmation that King Solomon upheld his father's proclamation to incorporate live praise during the services.

> **2 Chronicles 8:14-15** And, according to the order of David his father, he appointed the divisions of the priests for their service, the Levites for their duties (to praise and serve before the priests) as the duty of each day required, and the gatekeepers by their divisions at each gate; for so David the man of God had commanded. They did not depart from the command of the king to the priests and Levites concerning any matter or concerning the treasuries.

The instructions David received from the Lord to establish live praise during the services were also given to, and confirmed by, the prophets Gad and Nathan, this commandment was also maintained by Hezekiah with the restoration of the temple worship.

> **2 Chronicles 29:25-30** And he stationed the Levites in the house of the LORD with cymbals, with stringed instruments, and with harps, according to the commandment of David, of Gad the king's seer, and of Nathan the prophet; for thus *was* the commandment of the LORD by his prophets. The Levites stood with the instruments of David, and the priests with the trumpets. Then Hezekiah commanded *them* to offer the burnt offering on the altar. And when the burnt offering began, the song of the

LORD *also* began, with the trumpets and with the instruments of David king of Israel. So all the assembly worshiped, the singers sang, and the trumpeters sounded; all *this continued* until the burnt offering was finished. And when they had finished offering, the king and all who were present with him bowed and worshiped. Moreover King Hezekiah and the leaders commanded the Levites to sing praise to the LORD with the words of David and of Asaph the seer. So they sang praises with gladness, and they bowed their heads and worshiped.

We can clearly see as we read the preceding Scriptures that the Lord desired a live representation of the burning of incense. Through David He ordained the use of musical instruments, musicians, and singers to offer the sacrifice of praise, which we maintain in our services today.

CHAPTER TEN

PRAISE AT THE DEDICATION
OF SOLOMON'S TEMPLE

T he following Scriptures describe the day that Solomon's Temple was dedicated to the Lord. As you read them, pay special attention to the order of the events that took place. Sanctified priests brought the ark of the covenant to the Most Holy Place. Next, as they exited the inner sanctuary they were joined by many more priests, singers, musicians, and brethren. Together they united as one, to give thanks and to sing praises unto the Lord. Their praises were so intense and so heartfelt (pure incense), that God Himself, transformed their praise into a cloud that filled the temple, and so covered the mercy seat.

> **2 Chronicles 5:1,7,11-14** So all the work that Solomon had done for the house of the LORD was finished; and Solomon brought in the things which his father David had dedicated: the silver and the gold and all the furnishings. And he put *them* in the treasuries of the house of God. Then the priests brought in the ark of the covenant of the LORD to its

place, into the inner sanctuary of the temple, to the Most Holy *Place*, under the wings of the cherubim. And it came to pass when the priests came out of the *Most* Holy *Place* (for all the priests who *were* present had sanctified themselves, without keeping to their divisions), and the Levites *who were* the singers, all those of Asaph and Heman and Jeduthun, with their sons and their brethren, stood at the east end of the altar, clothed in white linen, having cymbals, stringed instruments and harps, and with them one hundred and twenty priests sounding with trumpets—indeed it came to pass, when the trumpeters and singers *were* as one, to make one sound to be heard in praising and thanking the LORD, and when they lifted up their voice with the trumpets and cymbals and instruments of music, and praised the LORD, *saying: "For He is* good, For His mercy *endures* forever,"* that the house, the house of the LORD, was filled with a cloud, so that the priests could not continue ministering because of the cloud; for the glory of the LORD filled the house of God.

When we read 2 Chronicles 6:19-42, we find confirmation that praise precedes prayer. Solomon lifted petitions for forgiveness and restoration, before the Lord, on behalf of the people after praises were lifted up, and the cloud covered the mercy seat (2 Chronicles 5). Praise is *required* by the Lord to precede prayer. Praise is the *key* that opens the door for prayers to be accepted into the presence of God and answered (2 Chronicles 7:1).

Consider the following illustration: there are precise laws of mathematics that must be followed, in the proper sequence, to calculate the right answer to a simple problem. For example, when solving (2+2x2=?), the laws of mathematics require that we first calculate the multiplication part of the problem followed next by the addition. When we follow the proper sequence, we will arrive at the correct answer, which is six. It may seem easier to do the addition first, but the end result will be the incorrect answer of eight.

Similarly, as in mathematics, there is always a correct order in which we should do things to solve life's problems successfully. Many people attempt to solve their problems by looking for the quickest, easiest way around them. The result of choosing a shortcut is often only a quick fix, a temporary solution that after time compounds the problem. It takes an earnest effort (work) to become a good problem solver. We must first seek good counsel. However, it is not enough to simply listen to counsel; we must carefully, attentively hear (heed) what we are taught. As we grasp good (right) knowledge and apply it to our lives, we will see the molehills that our quick fixes have made into mountains, crumble like sand beneath our feet. We find confirmation in the following Scripture that we should do things in the proper order.

> **Matthew 5:23-24** "Therefore if you bring your gift to the altar, and there remember that your brother has something against you, "leave your gift there before the altar, and go your way. First be reconciled to your brother, and then come and offer your gift.

As we read about the events that took place as King Solomon dedicated the temple, we saw that he followed the order of doing things that most pleased the Lord, by first praising and worshiping Him before entering into prayer. When the king finished lifting his prayer petitions, the glory of God fell from heaven and filled the temple, showing His good pleasure. "When Solomon had finished praying, fire came down from heaven and consumed the burnt offering and the sacrifices; and the glory of the LORD filled the temple" (2 Chronicles 7:1).

For generations to follow singers, accompanied by musicians, praised the Lord during temple services. King Hezekiah followed the example set by King David and then by King David's son, King Solomon, when he rededicated the temple to the Lord.

> **2 Chronicles 29:25-27** And he stationed the Levites in the house of the LORD with cymbals, with stringed instruments, and with harps, according to the commandment of David, of Gad the king's seer, and of Nathan the prophet; for thus *was* the commandment of the LORD by his prophets. The Levites stood with the instruments of David, and the priests with the trumpets. Then Hezekiah commanded *them* to offer the burnt offering on the altar. And when the burnt offering began, the song of the LORD *also* began, with the trumpets and with the instruments of David king of Israel.

CHAPTER ELEVEN

ATTITUDES TODAY
WORSHIP

S ince the sacrifice of Christ on the cross, the requirements to ready ourselves to enter the presence of God greatly differ from what was required by the high priest on the Day of Atonement. All the things that were done on the Day of Atonement were symbolic of the things to come and are written about in the Bible as examples for us. In this chapter we will take a closer look at those differences.

The high priest was required to perform certain rituals before he could enter into the presence of God with the blood for atonement. Only after he completed those rituals would he be allowed to safely enter and leave the Holy of Holies as often as it was necessary.

- First, from the congregation, he would select two goats as a sin offering and one ram as a burnt offering.
- He would then choose a bull as a sin offering for himself and his household.
- One of the two goats would be chosen to be killed and offered as a sin offering on the altar of burnt offerings.

The other goat was set free into the wilderness as a scape-goat, making atonement for the people.

- The priest would kill the bull and offer it on the altar of burnt offerings for his sins and for the sins of his household. (Some of the blood from the bull and the goat would be laid aside for the atonement, a censer would be filled with hot coals from the altar.)
- He would then wash himself and put on the required holy garments. One of the garments was the robe with golden bells (instruments of praise) attached to its hem, which would offer a continual sound of praise, allowing him to safely enter God's presence, "that he may not die."
- Next, he would enter the Holy of Holies, first with the censer filled with burning coals. He would then leave and return with his two hands full of incense which he was required to burn on the hot coals, so that a cloud of smoke would cover the mercy seat.
- Lastly, he would take the blood of the bull and so also the blood of the goat and re-enter the Holy of Holies to make atonement for the sins of himself, his family, and the people.

All of the preceding requirements that were necessary before the cross, to enter the presence of God to present the blood sacrifice for sin, have since been replaced with the following:

- Jesus, the Lamb of God, has replaced the bulls and the goats that were previously required for the atonement of our sins.
- The priest washing himself and putting on the holy garments has been replaced by us putting on a right frame of mind, and by focusing all of our thoughts on the Lord Jesus and on what He has done for us.

- The incense on the burning coals is now represented by the praises of our lips.
- The blood of the goats and bulls that was once required has been replaced by the precious blood of Jesus that was poured out at the cross.

When we come to church, we are in the outer court. When we focus on singing heartfelt praises unto Him, we are clothing ourselves in the garments of praise which takes us into the presence of the Lord.

Let us take a closer look at one of the requirements, putting on a right frame of mind:

> **Philippians 4:8** Finally, brethren, whatever things are true, whatever things *are* noble, whatever things *are* just, whatever things *are* pure, whatever things *are* lovely, whatever things *are* of good report, if *there is* any virtue and if *there is* anything praise-worthy—meditate on these things.

In this Scripture, God is requesting that we focus the thoughts of our daily lives on good things; how much more should we be in a right frame of mind when we desire the privilege of entering into His presence. Once we are in a right frame of mind we must worship the Lord in spirit and in truth by putting aside any thoughts that may distract us. This enables us to freely praise the Lord, which can lead us into an intimate moment with Him.

> **John 4:23-24** "But the hour is coming, and now is, when the true worshipers will worship the Father in spirit and truth; for the Father is seeking such to

worship Him. "God *is* Spirit, and those who worship Him must worship in spirit and truth."

Our Heavenly Father not only desires us to have the right frame of mind, He is seeking for "such" to worship Him in spirit and in truth. *The simplest expression of worship is* **acknowledgment.** When we bow our knees, in sincere prayer, we are worshiping. Prayer is an integral part of worship.

> **John 1:1-4** In the beginning was the Word, and the Word was with God, and the Word was God. He was in the beginning with God. All things were made through Him, and without Him nothing was made that was made. In Him was life, and the life was the light of men.

These verses are acknowledging the existence of God. They are declaring that God is life; that nothing can exist without Him; that He is our all in all. Here, the Word itself is worshiping God. Another example of the simplest form of worship can be found when we read Mark 5:1-7a. These Scriptures tell of a time when Jesus cast demons into swine. Let us look at verses 6 and 7a:

> **Mark 5:1-7a** Then they came to the other side of the sea, to the country of the Gadarenes. And when He had come out of the boat, immediately there met Him out of the tombs a man with an unclean spirit, who had *his* dwelling among the tombs; and no one could bind him, not even with chains, because he had often been bound with shackles and chains. And the chains had been pulled apart by him, and

the shackles broken in pieces; neither could anyone tame him. And always, night and day, he was in the mountains and in the tombs, crying out and cutting himself with stones. (6)When he saw Jesus from afar, he ran and worshiped Him. And he cried out with a loud voice and said, "What have I to do with You, Jesus, Son of the Most High God?"

When the demon man saw Jesus he "worshiped Him," he simply cried out, "Jesus, Son of the Most High God," *acknowledging* that Jesus is the Son of God.

When Jesus was led up by the Spirit, into the wilderness to be tempted by the devil, the devil asked the Son of God to worship him:

> **Matthew 4:8-9** Again, the devil took Him up on an exceedingly high mountain, and showed Him all the kingdoms of the world and their glory. And he said to Him, "All these things I will give You if You will fall down and worship me."

The devil wanted to be acknowledged (worshiped) by Jesus, for what he could offer Him. Instead, Jesus acknowledged His Father. *"You shall worship the LORD your God, and Him only you shall serve"* (Matthew 4:10b). His worship of God, His acknowledgement of His Father, caused Satan to depart from Him.

Worship is made all the more beautiful when we acknowledge His presence, His faithfulness, and our thankfulness in song, declaring with our lips all that God has done and is willing to do for us by His mercies and goodness. Praise cannot be separated from worship but worship can be separated from praise. Because when we **unconsciously** sing along, mechanically uttering words cannot take us into worshiping the Lord; it takes the **conscious willingness** of our hearts as we focus on the words we sing (present to Him) to accomplish that.

The word "spirit" denotes: a forcible respiration or breath; the life giving breath within us. He is seeking those who will worship Him (mindfully acknowledging His goodness), not allowing circumstances, problems, or emotions to encumber their thoughts. The enemy will attempt to distract us; he will bombard our minds with thoughts that will cause us to lose our focus. If we lose our focus while we are presenting our praises to the Lord, we must forcefully concentrate on refocusing all of our attention on Jesus. It is when we present heartfelt praise before the Lord that we are drawn into His presence.

The word "truth" means: to praise Him, truly and willingly from the heart, not ritualistically or unconsciously. While we are offering Him our sacrifice of praise, He should be the recipient of our undivided attention. The Father is seeking true worshipers, those who despite being in the midst of trials and tribulations, depend on the Spirit of the Lord for strength, and press in to worship (acknowledge) Him in spirit (forcefully) and in truth (truly, willingly). In other words, *acknowledge Him forcefully and willingly.*

David understood the Lord's limitless worth and how deserving He was to be praised. He removed his kingly robes and without shame, danced, leaped, and whirled before the Lord. David, the King of Israel, humbled himself before his Lord and the people. He did not hold back his praise from his beloved Lord; we should learn to do the same.

> **2 Samuel 6:14-15, 20-22** Then David danced before the LORD with all *his* might; and David *was* wearing a linen ephod. So David and all the house of Israel brought up the ark of the LORD with shouting and

with the sound of the trumpet. Then David returned to bless his household. And Michal the daughter of Saul came out to meet David, and said, "How glorious was the king of Israel today, uncovering himself today in the eyes of the maids of his servants, as one of the base fellows shamelessly uncovers himself!" So David said to Michal, "*It was* before the LORD, who chose me instead of your father and all his house, to appoint me ruler over the people of the LORD, over Israel. Therefore I will play *music* before the LORD. "And I will be even more **undignified** than this, and will be humble in my own sight. But as for the maidservants of whom you have spoken, by them I will be held in honor."

If you are still holding back your praise, or are offering it in reserved portions, for fear of appearing undignified, you have not yet come to the fullness of the realization of His immeasurable worth.

The marriage relationship between a husband and his wife is symbolic of the relationship between Jesus and the church (the bride). The great joy that a man and a woman experience, when by the unity of marriage they become one, symbolizes the joy we experience when we allow Jesus to come into our hearts. This is what the Holy Spirit is trying to reveal to us in Ephesians 5:31-32, "*For this reason a man shall leave his father and mother and be joined to his wife, and the two shall become one flesh.*" This is a great mystery, but I speak concerning Christ and the church."

After spending some time ministering to a precious sister in the Lord about the importance of worshiping the Lord in spirit and in truth, we spent some time reading about the Shulamite and the beloved in Song of Solomon. She took what she received during our Bible study and she presented me with the following story, written in her own words. She said it was meant to describe how she believes her husband must feel when she displays indifference towards him. It caused her to take a closer, more serious look at how she worships the Lord.

Imagine a married couple, each busy with the things of life. The husband rises early each morning and drives to work. He deals with the traffic and on some days, bad weather as well. Though his commute might be slow, his thoughts are racing. He is thinking about the bills that are piling up at home, the family's need for a more reliable second vehicle (so his wife can safely transport their children to and from their many activities), and his youngest child's need for braces. When he finally arrives at work he is informed at the morning meeting, that as the result of difficult economic times, the company must downsize at the end of the year. His day has barely begun and it has gone from bad to worse. He silently asks the Lord for favor in that situation and he proceeds with the work of the day, being sure to give it his best. As he punches his time card at the end of the day, he happily realizes it is Friday. During the drive home, he is comforted by thoughts of his wife. He wonders what kind of day she had. He hopes that she is at home when he arrives; he longs for her smile and her embrace. He pulls into the driveway as she is pulling out. She calls to him, telling him that dinner is in the oven and that she will be right back. She further explains that she is taking the children to her parents' house, just minutes away, for an overnight visit. His disappointment that she was leaving quickly changes to the hopeful anticipation of a quiet evening with her. He decides to quickly shower before she returns home. He is surprised when he finds himself singing as the thoughts of the stressed filled day have been replaced with thoughts of spending some much needed alone time with his wife. They enjoy a quiet dinner together and shortly afterwards decide to go to bed. As she is in the bathroom undressing, he is turning down their bed and lighting her favorite candles. Moments later they are together in bed and his every thought is of her, being with her...loving her...making her feel wanted and cared for...all the things he is hoping that she too is feeling about him. Consider how disheartened he felt when even though she was there physically, going through all the motions of intimacy, her thoughts were miles away; her focus was elsewhere. Something that should have been equally as meaningful to her was not. She did not purpose in her heart to focus all of her attention on her husband during their time of intimacy. She allowed what should have been precious moments spent with her husband to be robbed by the random thoughts of what lay ahead for her tomorrow.

When we do not worship the Lord in spirit and in truth, from our hearts, we too are displaying indifference (an uncaring, unappreciative, detached attitude). When we allow the enemy to distract us, we lose the opportunity to be blessed, healed, delivered, and strengthened, in essence, to be loved. To truly worship the Lord, in the manner He is worthy of, we must consciously purpose in our hearts to focus (and when we become distracted, to forcefully refocus) all of our attention on the words we sing, being mindful that we are presenting them to Him. Why is it so important for us to be consciously aware of the words we present before the Lord in song? Give some thought to the words we sing. They are usually words that declare our adoration, pledge our commitments, and present our vows (promises). They are often words of prayer; they should not be *casually* presented.

The Bible was not comprised of halfhearted, lukewarm words but instead with the mindfully authored written promises of God. Jesus gave His life to confirm His Word; He exalts His Word above His Holy name. How can we profess that we mean the words we sing if we are not making a purposeful effort to listen to them. Musical accompaniment helps us to lyrically (deeply, personally, emotionally) express our feelings, in songs of praise, towards the Lord. The psalms are prayers with lyrics; it is written in 1 Chronicles 16:9, "Sing to Him, sing psalms to Him." Consider the following verses:

> **Psalm 24:7-10** Lift up your heads, O you gates! And be lifted up, you everlasting doors! And the King of glory shall come in. Who *is* this King of glory? The LORD strong and mighty, The LORD mighty in battle. Lift up your heads, O you gates! Lift up, you everlasting doors! And the King of glory shall come in. Who is this King of glory? The LORD of hosts, He *is* the King of glory.

The King of Glory stands at the door of our hearts and knocks (Revelation 3:20). It is the desire of His heart, for us to welcome

Him in; He wants to provide our every need. As we lift our hands in praise, acknowledging His Holy presence, we will enter into the joy of the Lord. And as we truly worship, our hearts will open to welcome the Lord to enter and fill us with His strength, enabling us if we are willing to make changes in our lives. It is when we learn to live by His strength that we will see growth in our Christian walk.

The Lord has so many good thoughts about us, their number cannot be counted. He never leaves us or forsakes us; He inclines His ears to hear our every request. He longs for sweet fellowship with us. How must the Lord feel, when even in those few moments that we set aside to spend time with Him, to show Him how much we love Him with songs of adoration, we allow our thoughts to so easily wander to other things?

Now that we have taken a more in-depth look at putting on a right frame of mind, focusing our thoughts on Jesus and His worthiness to be praised, let us take a closer look at the requirement of entering the presence of God with the praise of our lips. "Therefore by Him let us continually offer the sacrifice of praise to God, that is, the **fruit** of *our* lips, giving thanks to His name" (Hebrews 13:15).

Here, once again, we are seeing that God desires the fruit of our lips to be continually giving thanks, as we lift Him up and envelope Him, in our sacrifice of praise. The simplest, and yet the greatest, form of giving thanks to God is to praise Him. Preparing ourselves with the right frame of mind, one that is ready to worship the Lord in spirit and truth, and continually offering the Lord the sacrifice of praise will enable us to enter God's presence whenever the need arises, just as David did. We can then lift up before Him, prayers for forgiveness, deliverance, and restoration on our own behalf or on behalf of others. We should always enter God's presence as David did, with the praises of our lips enveloping our prayers.

In His Word God gives us the following simple illustration: praise is *fruit,* it is the fruit of our lips. As a peach seed is enveloped by its fruit, our prayers should be enveloped by praises. The seed is hard and bitter. Many times praying may be difficult (hard) because we do not always know how to pray or what to pray about. The troubles of life that we sometimes find ourselves in, or the despair we experience when it *seems* our prayers are going unanswered, can be compared to the bitterness of the peach seed (pit). Yet, the peach seed needs to be planted to bring forth more fruit. Similarly, when we sow our prayers in our praises they will bring forth answers. Prayer is the seed of faith that once planted *will*, in due time, bear fruit. Just as the farmer who sows his seed into the ground must be patient and believe that his seeds will produce a crop, we too must be patient. We must believe as we sow our seeds of faith (prayer) into God's Kingdom, they will produce in God's perfect time, fruit (that which we have prayed for).

> **John 15:7-8** "If you abide in Me, and My words abide in you, you will ask what you desire, and it shall be done for you." By this My Father is glorified, that you bear much fruit; so you will be My disciples.

As the Lord of all creation enveloped the peach seed in a casing of sweet fruit and gave it to us, we should do the same by enveloping our prayers with the sweet incense of praise, the fruit of our lips, before we present them to Him. The psalms declare that praise looks good on us; praises are our garments. That is the reason that we witness miracles during so many praise and worship services. Countless miracles have happened during the praise and worship services of Kathryn Kuhlman (a tumor the size of a basketball falling off of someone's back, people leaping out of their wheelchairs, etc.).

When we share the testimonies of these miracles, God is glorified and our confidence in Him is strengthened. Let me take this opportunity to share one such testimony from our church.

There was an elderly woman who claimed that she was a member of our church; however, she never attended any of our services. Every few weeks she called the church to justify her absences. She explained that she suffered from serious arthritis and the pain caused her to wake between four and five every morning. To get relief from the pain she would take her medication. The pills would cause her to sleep beyond the time of our Sunday services; therefore, she never attended. As she was sharing this with me one day, I told her earnestly not to take those meds the following Sunday morning and to come to church no matter how difficult it may be. She heeded my counsel, and after attending her first service, which included praise and worship, she received a complete healing. She was never troubled by arthritis again. She was also dealing with a large tumor that visibly protruded from the left side of her throat/jaw line. Doctors considered surgically removing it but they were concerned that there might be complications due to her age. During her third or fourth Sunday attendance at our church, very close to the end of *praise and worship*, I felt someone grab my hand. It was her; she was jabbing my hand to her throat and shouting excitedly, *It is gone! It is gone!* The tumor had miraculously disappeared. She received her second miracle on the heels of her first, both while in the midst of the sacrifice of praise to the Lord.

There have also been miracles at the praise and worship services of other ministers before they even stood to preach.

*God is glorified and miracles take place during
the times when His people assemble to praise Him.*

CHAPTER TWELVE

SET FREE BY THE TRUTH

In the same way the farmer with the peach seed must be patient and believe that once he plants his seed in good ground that it will (in the right season) produce fruit, we too by faith must believe the same thing about our prayers. When we speak them before a merciful God and we envelop them in praise, they too are falling on good ground, and in God's perfect time (good season), they will come to fruition. If the farmer were to become impatient or doubtful that he had not properly planted his seed the first time, causing him to dig it up and replant it a second time, it would only result in compromising the integrity of the seed. The farmer can not predict precisely when his seeds will sprout life. In the same way we can not know exactly when our prayers will be answered; but they *will* be answered. Praying repeatedly for the same thing does not increase the prayer's potential to be answered. Instead, it reduces us to begging and affects the results/outcome of our prayers.

Many years ago, when I first came to live in the United States, I met a woman who was an intercessor; we became close friends. She telephoned me one day and shared with me that she had been dealing with an ailment that was causing her great pain. She was suffering both physically and emotionally because she had prayed to be healed and could not understand why the Lord had not yet answered her prayer. I asked her, *How often have you prayed for a healing for that specific ailment?* She answered, *Almost daily.* When I heard her answer I knew that her repetitive praying was nullifying the power of her initial prayer.

It brought back to my remembrance a time in the past when I would lead the church in prayer, according to my prior understanding of how to pray. The hour I spent in prayer would become tiresome and difficult. This was compounded by a troublesome period in my own life; thankfully the Lord separated me from what I was doing and He began to show me the proper way to pray. It was during this time of separation that He told me that each time I repeated a prayer I was actually nullifying my original request. I shared with her the following, simple but enlightening, illustration that the Lord gave to me when I was having difficulty praying because I too, was repeating prayers.

A young child asks her adoptive mother if she may have a glass of milk. Her mother anticipated her daughter's need for milk and had purchased it earlier, so she willingly responds, *Yes, you may.* The mother pours a glass of milk and sets it on the counter. A few minutes later the child asks a second time for a glass of milk. Her mother seeing that she has yet to drink the glass of milk she had already poured, turns to her daughter and answers once again, *Yes child, the milk is there for you to drink.* A short time later, the daughter asks her mother a third time for a glass of milk. By this time her mother was becoming frustrated with her daughter's continual asking and even more frustrated with the child's distrust and disbelief that it was her *will* for her daughter to have the milk she so desired.

As the result of the child's past (she was abandoned by her birth parents and abused in orphanages and foster homes), she had to learn to trust in the goodness of her adoptive mother. Before we even ask, the Lord knows our needs; just as the mother knew her daughter would need milk and willingly provided it for her, how much more should we know our God has willingly provided all our needs (Matthew 7:11). The child in the story reverted to begging her mother for milk even though her request was heard and answered *Yes* the first time. The Lord hears our prayers the first time we ask and He is faithful to provide our needs; when we ask more than once we are displaying, like the child in the story, a distrusting, unbelieving, worrisome heart. When we accept the Lord Jesus into our hearts, we are freed by the "Spirit of adoption" from worrying about our lives. We no longer have to be like the heathen (unbelievers). "For you did not receive the spirit of bondage again to fear, but you received the Spirit of adoption by whom we cry out, "Abba, Father" (Romans 8:15).

Before we utter a single word in prayer our Heavenly Father knows each and every one of our needs, and since He did not withhold His only Son, but freely gave Him for our sins, how much more does He desire to freely give us all things (Romans 8:32). However, it is not enough to simply ask (pray); the power to receive comes when we maintain our faith (hold on to our confidence) in God and in His faithfulness to provide all things that pertain to life. We demonstrate our faith by our willingness to praise God, when we wholeheartedly give thanks, believing that those things that we have lifted before His Throne of Grace, will come to fruition. Consider the following:

A child, from a home of modest means, asks his loving father if he could have a new bicycle. The father wanted his son to have a new bike but knew that finances were limited; he explained to his son that he was expecting a bonus in four weeks and at that time he would buy him a new bike. The child now having a hope in his heart did not ask his father a second time. Instead, to show his appreciation, he willingly did all his chores and with a genuine heart, he praised and loved on his father while he waited. He acted as if he had already received the new bike. He trusted in the word of his father and his confidence in that word was proven by his grateful heart. While he waited for his father to receive his bonus, he boldly announced to the neighborhood children that he would soon have a new bicycle. The children, in response, demonstrated their disbelief by taunting and teasing the boy, declaring that he would not really be getting a new bike. The child was presented with a decision to make. Would he allow the doubts of his *friends* to cause him to lose confidence in the word of his father, or would he hold tight to the conviction of his heart and continue to stand on the promise of his loving father's word? The boy decided to reject the doubts and he purposed in his heart not to ask again. He shared with his father how the other children had been teasing him and how painful it had been for him to hear all their words of disbelief, making the waiting difficult, but he assured his father that he remained confident that he would receive what he had been promised. It is written, "...do not become sluggish, but imitate those who through faith and patience inherit the promises" (Hebrews 6:12). The father comforted his son by telling him how good it made him feel that he believed in him and that he would do everything possible to see that he received his new bike. He thanked (praised) his father and found comfort (peace) while he continued to wait. The boy's father was touched by his son's trust, and knowing that he had endured painful taunting from his friends, happily looked forward to presenting him with the new bike.

It is okay to share our pains with God, but we must be careful not to allow the enemy to cause us, in our sorrows, to cast aside our confidence in Him. On the night before His crucifixion, Jesus told His Father of His sorrows, the difficulties He was facing, yet He never uttered doubts. He knew what He had to do; even unto death He held fast to His faith in God.

> **Matthew 26:36-39** Then Jesus came with them to a place called Gethsemane, and said to the disciples, "Sit here while I go and pray over there." And He took with Him Peter and the two sons of Zebedee, and He began to be sorrowful and deeply distressed. Then He said to them, "My soul is exceedingly sorrowful, even to death. Stay here and watch with Me." He went a little farther and fell on His face, and prayed, saying, "O My Father, if it is possible,

let this cup pass from Me; nevertheless, not as I will, but as You *will*."

It is so very important that we learn to pray in the way that most pleases the Father. We can, as Jesus did in the preceding prayer, find peace, comfort, and strength for all situations when we pray. In the following chapter we will take a closer, more in depth look at how we should pray for ourselves, how to intercede on behalf of others, and how to add the power of fasting to our prayers.

CHAPTER THIRTEEN

PRAYER

DO NOT BE REPETITIOUS

Many people mistakenly assume that the more words they speak while praying, the better their chances are for a favorable response. Unfortunately, what often happens is, the wordier our prayers become, the more they tend to be repetitious. The word "repetition" is derived from the Greek word *battologeo*. Its many meanings include: not to speak negatively, angrily, unadvisedly; to babble as if stammering; being repetitive yet unclear. God is neither deaf nor forgetful and when we repeat our prayers we are displaying a lack of faith; we are declaring that we do not believe He heard us the first time. Our prayers should be specific and to the point and most importantly they should be asked only *once*. Repetition robs us of our confidence; it fills our hearts with fear and doubt. Jesus Himself taught us how to pray during His *Sermon on the Mount* (Matthew 6:5-13).

> **Matthew 6:7-8** "And when you pray, do not use **vain repetitions** as the heathen *do*. For they think that they will be heard for their many words. "Therefore

do not be like them. For your Father knows the things you have need of before you ask Him."

In the preceding verses, Jesus is clearly teaching His disciples (students, followers of His Word), both then and now, not to repeat prayers. Before we utter a single word the Lord knows the things that we are in need of, so we should keep our prayers precise. Our prayers should plainly declare our needs, regardless of what they are for : forgiveness, healing, deliverance, wisdom, strength, direction in life, success, etc. When we pray, we should use the words the Lord used in the promises He made to us in the Bible.

Some people use the *Parable of the Persistent Widow*, in Luke 18 as justification to repeat their prayers. They believe that the woman in the story received a favorable decision from the unjust judge because she repeatedly *asked* him for justice. The Bible does *not* contradict itself; God is not the author of confusion. Prior to sharing the parable, Jesus declared that we should *always pray and do not lose heart*. The Lord wants us to pray *continually, not repeatedly* ("...you do not have because you do not ask" James 4:2b) and He does not want us to cast aside (give up) our confidence in His Word. Let us take a closer look at the parable:

> **Luke 18:2-8** "There was in a certain city a judge who did not fear God nor regard man." Now there was a widow in that city; and she came to him, saying, 'Get justice for me from my adversary.' "And he would not for a while; but afterward he said within himself, 'Though I do not fear God nor regard man, 'yet because this widow troubles me I will avenge her, lest by her continual coming she weary me.'" Then the Lord said, "Hear what the unjust judge said. "And shall God not avenge His own elect who

cry out day and night to Him, though He bears long with them? "I tell you that He will avenge them speedily. Nevertheless, when the Son of Man comes, will He really find faith on the earth?"

The Lord uses this parable to emphasize the confidence the woman displayed because she believed, that sooner or later, her case would be heard. She knew that even though her petition was presented before an unjust judge, she would in the end receive justice. The widow had a hope and she exhibited that hope by continually coming; it was that persistence and the way she steadfastly held on to her confidence, not allowing herself to be turned away as the days dragged on, that empowered her to repeatedly return to the courthouse. The word "persist" means: to continue steadily or firmly in spite of opposition; to last or endure; to be insistent. She would sit in the presence of the judge, waiting for him to arbitrate (handle) her case. Growing weary of her "continual coming," he ordered that her case be brought before him; he wanted to rule on it and be rid of her. If he had been a God-fearing righteous judge, he would have dispensed justice when she initially presented her petition and her persistent coming would not have been necessary. In the parable, Jesus reminds us (His elect) that He will undoubtedly and "speedily" avenge us.

The Word of God commands judges to fear God. It is that fear that motivates obedience; for whom we fear we will obey. Judges are the earthly vessels that occupy God's seat on earth for the purpose of passing down judgments on His people. God's Word declares that judges should deliver the poor, the needy, the oppressed, and most especially, the widows and orphans. They must not show favoritism or accept bribes. They must at all times remain impartial as not to pass down corrupt judgments. The wicked judge in the parable did not fear God; his actions were in direct opposition to God's Word. If we hold on to our confidence we will see what we have asked and what we are waiting for come to pass. If we cast aside our confidence, we are casting aside our faith and hope. The last line of the parable confirms exactly that, "Nevertheless, when the Son of Man comes, will He really find faith on earth?"

Another parable that is often mistakenly used to support the validity that repetition is acceptable is the *Parable of the Persistent Friend.*

> **Luke 11:5-10** And He said to them, "Which of you shall have a friend, and go to him at midnight and say to him, 'Friend, lend me three loaves; 'for a friend of mine has come to me on his journey, and I have nothing to set before him'; "and he will answer from within and say, 'Do not trouble me; the door is now shut, and my children are with me in bed; I cannot rise and give to you'? "I say to you, though he will not rise and give to him because he is his friend, yet because of his **persistence** he will rise and give him as many as he needs. "So I say to you, ask, and it will be given to you; seek, and you will find; knock, and it will be opened to you. "For everyone who asks receives, and he who seeks finds, and to him who knocks it will be opened.

In this story the Lord is once again telling us not to allow anyone, anything, or any circumstance to deter or stop us from making an important or urgent request. If the man in the parable had accepted his friend's initial response, he would have returned home to his hungry visitor empty-handed. It was his *persistence* which kept him from being turned away and which ultimately convinced his friend to rise from his warm bed to meet his need. The Word encourages us to ask, to seek, and to knock. There may be times when we seek assistance from our friends and they are reluctant to extend their help; it may be necessary to remind them of times when their needs were willingly met by others. The bold among us might even challenge a friend by saying, *I heard your cry, why are you turning a deaf ear to mine?* A true friend would not purposefully deny us, but he or she may not always give our pleas enough consideration before responding. If the man in the parable had thoughtfully considered that his friend had left his home late at night, forsaking his own comfort and rest, to meet a need that was not even his own (a friend had arrived unexpectedly, at his home, weary and *hungry* after traveling far on foot, during perilous after dark hours), he surely would have given his friend a few loaves straightaway. The Lord uses this parable to teach that we should continue to press in, even when the situation *seems* fruitless. It is that same kind of persistence that is confirmed in the following:

> **Matthew 20:29-34** Now as they went out of Jericho, a great multitude followed Him. And behold, two blind men sitting by the road, when they heard that Jesus was passing by, cried out, saying, "Have mercy on us, O Lord, Son of David!" Then the multitude warned them that they should be quiet; but they cried out all the more, saying, "Have mercy on us, O Lord, Son of David!" So Jesus stood still and called them, and said, "What do you want Me to do for you?" They said to Him, "Lord, that our eyes may be opened." So Jesus had compassion and touched their eyes. And immediately their eyes received sight, and they followed Him.

In spite of being greatly outnumbered and warned that they should remain quiet the two blind men, knowing that they had a great need and not wanting their only hope to pass them by, persistently cried out all the more. Jesus, hearing them, stopped and asked, "What do you want Me to do for you?" They presented their need (they asked only once) and Jesus was faithful to meet it. Similarly, in Luke, chapters 7 and 8, we can read about two women whose boldness and perseverance enabled one to receive forgiveness for her morally corrupt lifestyle and the other to receive a much needed healing from the issue of blood. The enemy will use every opportunity that arises to chisel away at our faith. He knows that if we press in and make our needs known to God that God *will* be faithful to provide them. The enemy devises ways to intimidate us and to make us feel unworthy; he overwhelms us with thoughts that our situation is too impossible to overcome. When we allow the enemy to cause us to become fearful or to become uncertain or hesitant, the result is a shaken confidence. When we submit to the will of the enemy, he is glorified.

I would like to share with you a personal testimony about a time in my life when what seemed to be an impossible endeavor was made possible through perseverance.

It was just a few days before I was scheduled to leave for Africa to share the Lord's message on the importance of praise enveloping prayer. I was closing a prayer service at my church when the Lord spoke to me saying, *You do not have a passport.* When I arrived home, I confirmed what the Lord had spoken; my passport had expired. This was my dilemma. It was Thursday evening and I was leaving for Africa first thing Monday morning. I could only obtain a new passport from one place, the Dutch Embassy, in

New York City, and I had only one day to accomplish that. Believing that with God all things are possible, I said a simple prayer and made plans to make the three hour drive to New York early the next morning. My wife, Stella, accompanied me. We arrived at the embassy at 7am, two hours before it opened, and we were the first ones in line at 9am. I presented my letter of invitation from my African colleague, my travel itinerary, my airline ticket, and my expired passport to the window clerk. I explained my situation and remained hopeful that she would help me. She said, without hesitation, *It is impossible to process a passport in just a few hours. It will take at least two weeks.* Because of my continued persistence, she went to confer with the consul who sent her back to tell me that he would make an exception, but that Monday would be the earliest a new passport could be processed. I knew that I could not accept that response because it would mean missing my flight which would greatly affect my plans. I tried to convince her not to dismiss my request so quickly, *There must be something you can do.* My persistence seemed to be of no avail, so I asked if I could speak to the consul. She said that he was too busy at the moment to see me. I decided to wait, so my wife and I stepped out of the line and found a place to sit. We waited for hours. We watched as everyone left for lunch and then returned. The attendants periodically checked to see if we were still waiting. As we exchanged glances, some seemed to suggest that we were wasting our time, while others seemed to show sympathy for our patient persistence. We continued to be hopeful even as we watched them close their windows for business. Our efforts eventually proved fruitful; it seemed that they had grown tired of seeing us sitting there and at about 3pm, the consul finally agreed to issue me a temporary passport (a pink covered one) similar to the type that would be issued to someone who has lost their passport in a foreign country. Three days later, I left for Africa as I had originally planned.

Throughout the time we waited we did not repeat our prayer, instead we remained hopeful, continually giving thanks, knowing that we will never be disappointed when we put our hope in the Lord. Unlike our prayers, which should never be repeated, expressions of *confidence* in His promises are always worth repeating.

The following is yet another example of persistence prevailing over simply accepting *No* for an answer:

The year is 1956; the place is a public library in a small town in Georgia (USA). An eight year old boy is standing on his tip toes, determined to reach the librarian's counter. *May I help you?* a stern voice asks. The boy excitedly answers, *Yes, ma'am. I would like to take this book home. I mean, I would like to check it out*, he quickly corrects himself. *I'm sorry, that is impossible,* the woman responds. *Why?* asks the boy. *Can't you read?* she replies. *Sure I can. That's why I want to check out this book,* he proudly answers. The librarian points to a sign that is hanging over the door. *Read that!* The young boy carefully reads the words etched into the sign: White people ONLY are permitted to check out books. *Ma'am, when will black people be permitted to check out books?* the boy asks. *When the law changes! Now move along!* she barks. He gives her answer some thought and then politely declares, *Then I guess I will just have to stay here and wait.* She grumbles impatiently, *Young man, that could take some time.* He quickly replies, *That's okay. I have lots of time and you have lots of books that I can read while I wait.* The boy steps away from the counter and sits on the floor, being sure to remain in her line of vision. He quietly reads his book over and over, and whenever he catches her glaring at him, he smiles at her. Eventually, she grew tired of seeing him there. His persistence wore her down. As he quietly held on to his hope, her blood pressure rose to its boiling point. The boy found victory that day as he happily left the library with a skip in his step and the book, that the librarian reluctantly allowed him to check out, tucked securely under his arm.

Everyone of us has experienced a time when we were given *No* for an answer and were presented with an opportunity to either hold onto our hope, by pressing in to find victory, or to give up our hope and simply accept defeat. For example, many of us have experienced the following:

A time presents itself when it is necessary to purchase a new vehicle. After predetermining which car you want to buy and how much you can afford to pay for it, you go to the dealership. Upon arriving, an eager salesman greets you and asks if he can be of any help. You tell him which car you want to buy and what you are prepared to pay for it. The sales-man responds, almost laughingly, telling you that the amount you have stated does not even come close to the sticker price of the car. You, knowing that he is trying to both intimidate you and pro-tect his commission, tell him that you do not want to waste his time and you would appreciate him not wasting yours. Seeing that you are serious, he excuses himself to speak to his manager. Minutes later he returns with a counteroffer slightly lower than the car's sticker price, but you are sure he can do better. You are now presented with a decision to make. Do you accept this new offer that is still more than you want to pay or do you press in and ask to speak to the sales manager yourself? Those of us who have made the decision not to settle but to instead persevere, have often times found that because of our persistence we prevailed. Does any of the following sound familiar? You decide to ask to speak with the manager; he comes out to see you and tries to convince you that the dealership would suffer a loss if it were to accept any less for the car than its last offer. You continue to hold on to your belief that not only *can* the dealership meet your price but if you do not relent, they *will* meet it. Real-izing that you now need some leverage, you tell the manager, *If your last offer is your final offer, let me not take up any more of your time. I'll try the dealership down the street.* Recognizing that you will not be moved to pay any more for the car than your initial offer, and not wanting to lose the sale to a competi-tor, the manager is now ready to agree to your price.

Secretly knowing that your offer will still make a profit for the dealership, but wanting to *save face* he replies, *I really cannot accept any less for the car, but let me take another look at your trade-in, maybe I can give you more for that.* (Receiving more for your trade-in would be a roundabout way to lower the cost of the car.) Or perhaps they offer you an interest rate that is less than you were able to secure from your bank, which ultimately reduces the final cost of the car. Possibly you have heard this, *I can offer you our repeat customer discount if anyone in your family has purchased a car from us in the past.* Feeling victorious as you leave with the keys to your new car in hand, you realize that it's not important *how* the dealership met your price, but that because of your persistence you prevailed.

Our God wants to meet our every need and in doing so He is showing us that He is a good God and He alone is worthy to be glorified. "And whatever you ask in My name, that I will do, that the Father may be glorified in the Son" (John 14:13). There are no limitations to what He is able to do for us. It is we who limit Him, especially when we hold back our petitions. It is written in John 15:7b, "you will ask what you desire, and it shall be done for you." The words "you will ask" denote: confidence, and the word "done" means: to be created; to come into being; arise be assembled, be fulfilled.

When we read John 11, we will see others in the Word whose lack of faith caused Jesus to groan in the spirit. The chapter details a time when Jesus was summoned by Mary and Martha to Judea to heal their sick brother Lazarus. Jesus had crossed over the Jordan, where John had baptized, and was ministering there when the news of Lazarus' sickness reached Him. After praying about the situation, Jesus sent word to the two women that the outcome of their brother's illness would not be death. "This sickness is not unto death, but for the glory of God, that the Son of God may be glorified through it" (John 11:4). The word "glorified" in the verse means: proven to be a good God. Jesus did not go immediately to Judea. He continued to minister for two more days, knowing that the sickness would not ultimately claim the life of Lazarus, because He would raise him from his death.

Before Jesus cried out, "Lazarus, come forth!" at the tomb where he lay dead for four days, He repeated His earlier prayer to the Father. Jesus repeated His prayer solely for the benefit of the people who witnessed it, to help strengthen their faith in God.

> **John 11:41b-42** And Jesus lifted up *His* eyes and said, "Father, I thank You that You have heard Me.
> "And I know that You always hear Me, but because of the people who are standing by I said *this*, that they may believe that You sent Me."

We have this same legal right, it is written in the Bible, that when we pray, standing on the promises of His Word, God inclines (spreads out) His ears to hear our prayers. We too, can declare with confidence that God always hears our prayers. We should never have to be repetitious when praying; God always hears us the first time. When we are repetitious we are displaying a lack of faith in God's Word. When we repeat our prayers we are denying the faith we have, that God always hears us, and that He knows our needs, and wants to provide them. Praising the Lord before we lift our petitions, and continually after, would be better use of our time. Praising God serves a manifold purpose:

it glorifies God; it brings peace to the worshiper by diminishing feelings of guilt, fear, and doubt; and it brings a calm assurance while we are waiting for the answers to our prayers. If you are able, you may also spend some time praying in the Holy Spirit, for this will also build up your faith. "But you, beloved, building yourselves up on your most holy faith, praying in the Holy Spirit" (Jude 20).

We should not be like the prophets of Baal and Asherah (heathen). It is written in 1 Kings 18, that the prophets of Baal called on him from morning to evening, repeating their petition for him to put fire under their sacrifice. They even went as far as to leap about the altar they made and cut themselves, and still they received no response from Baal. Elijah, the prophet of the Lord, mocked them and said, "Cry aloud, for he *is* a god; either he is meditating, or he is busy, or he is on a journey, *or* perhaps he is sleeping and must be awakened" (1 Kings 18:27b). We serve the God of Israel, who unlike Baal, neither sleeps nor slumbers, and whose ears and eyes are continually with us. We have to trust, as Elijah did, in God's Word; we should call on God with each petition only once, believing He has heard us and knowing that He will be faithful to answer.

> **Matthew 7:9-11** "Or what man is there among you who, if his son asks for bread, will give him a stone?
> "Or if he asks for a fish, will he give him a serpent?
> "If you then, being evil, know how to give good gifts to your children, how much more will your Father who is in heaven give good things to those who ask Him!

Here the Lord is using this simple parable to show us that if we, being mere human and evil in nature, know how to give our children, in their times of need, good things (things that sustain life) how much more should we trust that our Father in heaven, whose nature is pure goodness, will give to all who ask of Him the best of every good thing.

* * *

INTERCESSION

What is intercession? Intercession is a prayer or petition lifted to God on behalf of another person. It is when we *earnestly* pray for the benefit of someone else, for the purpose of changing the negative outcome that the course of their life, if left unchanged, is sure to produce. It is when we stand in the gap for another person, by entreating (pleading, imploring, appealing) before God the Father, for the sole purpose of moving on His mercy to forgive them, heal them, restore them, or deliver them (whatever their need may be). It is written, "...pray for one another, that you may be healed. The effective, fervent prayer of a righteous man avails much" (James 5:16b). An "effective, fervent prayer" is an *earnest* prayer.

Intercession is an awesome act of selflessness, motivated by the love intercessors have in their hearts for Jesus. Intercession is the willing sacrifice of oneself for the benefit of another; it is giving of your life to see the promises of God fulfilled in someone else's life. Intercessors intercede with Jesus for the salvation of others; they willingly forsake their own comfort while praying and/or fasting, by going without sleep and/or food.

The Holy Spirit intercedes for us, He mediates to the Father on our behalf; He knows what we will be in need of, before the need arises.

Romans 8:26-27 Likewise the Spirit also helps in our weaknesses. For we do not know what we should pray for as we ought, but the Spirit Himself makes intercession for us with groanings which cannot be uttered. Now He who searches the hearts knows what the mind of the Spirit *is*, because He makes intercession for the saints according to *the will of* God.

All Christians are called to be intercessors, to stand in the gap for someone else. When we know of someone who is in a weakened state, because the enemy has a hold on an area of their life, we need to stand by that person. We should lift them up in prayer, regardless of whether they are *friend or foe*. God is pleased when we call on Him in prayer, especially when we are giving of our lives for the wellbeing of others.

Another form of intercession is when we take it upon ourselves to release another person from a debt they cannot pay, one that would result in the loss of their freedom (example: paying fines imposed as a result of breaking the law). Is that not what Jesus did for us? He took our sins (our debts) to the cross, dying in our place, paying the ultimate price for our freedom; a price we, ourselves could never pay? This is the highest form of intercession.

If after awhile, a situation that an intercessor(s) has lifted in prayer seems unchanged or perhaps has even worsened but there are no new developments concerning the petition to pray about, it is important for the intercessor(s) to continue to stand on the original prayer. It is true that the waiting can sometimes seem long and tedious, and the enemy will do his best to convince us that our prayers will remain unanswered, but the intercessor(s) must not repeat their prayer or ask someone else to pray for them. Instead, while waiting for their prayer to be manifested they should use their time wisely. Set aside time to praise the Lord; play praise music and sing praises, giving Him thanks for His mercies and His faithfulness to watch over His Word to perform it. Spend some time praying in the Holy Spirit. Become radical; add the power of fasting to your praises, showing compassion for one another.

Yet another form of intercession is when we add fasting to our fervent praying, while we are waiting to see our prayers on behalf of others come to fruition. There is added power when we deny ourselves food; food is life's greatest pleasure as well as its greatest necessity.

Prayer of agreement: Standing alone while we are waiting to see a prayer answered, whether it is a prayer that we have lifted on our own behalf or one lifted on behalf of another, can sometimes be difficult. Having someone stand with you is not only comforting but it strengthens you while you wait. The Word confirms that our strength is increased when we stand together, "Though one may be overpowered by another, two can withstand him. And a threefold cord is not quickly broken" (Ecclesiastes 4:12). When we ask another to stand with us, united in agreement, believing that the prayer that was lifted will come to pass, those standing with us do not need to repeat the petition that was already asked. They need only recognize that the Lord has already heard the request and when we speak it a second time, it is for their benefit (as Jesus did at the resurrection of Lazarus). How can they stand in agreement if they do not know what they are agreeing to?

An example of a simple prayer of agreement would be as follows: *Father, we have come to lift before you Sarah, and her need to be healed from cancer. We know that by the stripes of Jesus, she has already been healed. We are lifting this prayer a second time, not because we do not believe that You heard this prayer the first time it was presented, and not because we are not confident that Your answer was already "Yes and Amen," but we do so to lend our support to our sister while she waits to see Your Word performed in her life. We come to give You thanks for your mercy, for Sara's healing, and for Your continual faithfulness. This we do in the name of Your Son, Jesus. Amen.*

*Know that you are never alone while you
wait. He is with you; He will strengthen you.*

* * *

FASTING

Fasting is based on the principle of giving, "Give, and it will be given to you…" We prove our love for one another as we fast (lay our lives down) for each other. "This is My commandment, that you love one another as I have loved you. "Greater love has no one than this, than to lay down one's life for his friends" (John 15:12-13). Fasting adds power to intercessory prayer. God honors the sacrifices of our flesh especially when they are made for the benefit of others. We should fast because we know that fasting, together with fervent prayer, has the power to break the yokes (the bonds) of oppression. We should fast for those we see struggling to find freedom or deliverance from a negative situation or difficulty (weakness). "*Is* this not the fast that I have chosen: To loose the bonds of wickedness, To undo the heavy burdens, To let the oppressed go free, And that you break every yoke?" (Isaiah 58:6).

Fasting is not for the purpose of displaying a show of *humility* that others may come to know that we are fasting. "Is it a fast that I have chosen, A day for a man to afflict his soul? *Is it* to bow down his head like a bulrush, And to spread out sackcloth and ashes?

Would you call this a fast, And an acceptable day to the LORD?" (Isaiah 58:5). While we are abstaining from food we should not act as self-appointed martyrs that draw attention to themselves. When we fast openly, allowing others to take notice of our sacrifice, we diminish the power and the purpose of the fast. Only our Heavenly Father should know of our sacrifice; it is His approval we should seek. He will be faithful to answer our prayers and to bless our selfless acts.

> **Matthew 6:16-18** "Moreover, when you fast, do not be like the hypocrites, with a sad countenance. For they disfigure their faces that they may appear to men to be fasting. Assuredly, I say to you, they have their reward. "But you, when you fast, anoint your head and wash your face, "so that you do not appear to men to be fasting, but to your Father who *is* in the secret *place;* and your Father who sees in secret will reward you openly.

Humility is not an outward expression of passiveness or piety; it is a decision to do what is required of you contrary to the internal or expressed emotions you may be experiencing.

Fasting is primarily ordained for the benefit of others. However, there are acceptable reasons to fast for oneself: to add sincerity to our prayers (when asking the Lord for help to make a moral change); for medical reasons (health benefits, blood tests, impending surgery); to lose weight (dieting); or to show the seriousness of one's commitment (for instance, when seeking to join various Christian organizations). These are acceptable reasons to fast, but they are all still motivated by self-benefit. Only **one** fast was chosen by the Lord, and it is the only **one** that has the power to provide freedom for others (Isaiah 58:6).

In the Bible we can find clear examples of true fasts that had powerful results. Let us first look at the Book of Esther. Esther knew that Haman had cunningly persuaded the king to decree the annihilation of all the Jews who were found living in the kingdom's provinces. She wanted to save her people and she knew she would have to meet with the king, hoping against hope that she could convince him to reverse his order. At that time there was an edict (law) in place; it called for anyone who entered the inner court of the king *unsummoned* to be put to death unless the king held out the golden scepter granting them entrance and sparing their lives. It had been a month since Esther had last been called before the king. She called for a fast to stay (suspend) the law so she might be granted the opportunity to present Haman's evil plans to the king.

> **Esther 4:15-16** Then Esther told *them* to reply to Mordecai: "Go, gather all the Jews who are present in Shushan, and fast for me; neither eat nor drink for three days, night or day. My maids and I will fast likewise. And so I will go to the king, which *is* against the law; and if I perish, I perish!"

Esther's life, as well as the lives of her people, was spared and Haman's evil plans were exposed.

> **Esther 7:9-10** Now Harbonah, one of the eunuchs, said to the king, "Look! The gallows, fifty cubits high, which Haman made for Mordecai, who spoke good on the king's behalf, is standing at the house of Haman." Then the king said, "Hang him on it!" So

they hanged Haman on the gallows that he had prepared for Mordecai. Then the king's wrath subsided.

In Daniel 9, we can read about another powerful fast that took place in the first year of King Darius' reign. After seeing it written that Jerusalem would lay in waste for seventy years and realizing that, that period of time had already been fulfilled, Daniel initiated a fast to break the decree (the yoke) issued by King Artaxerxes (Ezra 4). That decree had halted the first attempt to rebuild the temple during the reign of King Cyrus (Ezra 1). Acting as an intercessor, Daniel fasted and called upon the Lord to have mercy on all of Israel. Because of Daniel's willingness to lay his life down for others, to stand on God's Word, holding Him accountable to His Word, the Lord called him, "O Daniel, man greatly beloved."

> **Daniel 9:3-4** Then I set my face toward the Lord God to make request by prayer and supplications, with fasting, sackcloth, and ashes. And I prayed to the LORD my God, and made confession, and said, "O Lord, great and awesome God, who keeps His covenant and mercy with those who love Him, and with those who keep His commandments..."

Yet another fast found in the Word, one that exemplifies the power of praise when it is combined with prayer, is documented in 2 Chronicles. Knowing that an attack from a great multitude of armies from several nations was impending, and realizing that they did not have the strength or the power to defeat their enemies, Jehoshaphat proclaimed a fast. "And Jehoshaphat feared, and set himself to seek the LORD, and proclaimed a fast throughout all Judah" (2 Chronicles 20:3). The Lord responded to the fast and to the prayers of the King through Jahaziel; "And he said,

'Listen, all you of Judah and you inhabitants of Jerusalem, and you, King Jehoshaphat! Thus says the LORD to you: 'Do not be afraid nor dismayed because of this great multitude, for the battle *is* not yours, but God's" (2 Chronicles 20:15). Jehoshaphat appointed those who should sing to the Lord, praising the beauty of His holiness, as they led the army. They sang, "Praise the LORD, For His mercy *endures* forever" (2 Chronicles 20:21b).

> **2 Chronicles 20:22-24** Now when they began to sing and to praise, the LORD set ambushes against the people of Ammon, Moab, and Mount Seir, who had come against Judah; and they were defeated. For the people of Ammon and Moab stood up against the inhabitants of Mount Seir to utterly kill and destroy *them*. And when they had made an end of the inhabitants of Seir, they helped to destroy one another. So when Judah came to a place overlooking the wilderness, they looked toward the multitude; and there *were* their dead bodies, fallen on the earth. No one had escaped.

Without raising a single weapon to defend themselves, their enemies were defeated by the power of God that caused them to turn on one another; not one of the great multitude survived. Throughout the Bible, we can find additional accounts of times when fasting had the power to stop what the enemy meant for wrong; see the lives of David, Ezra, Jeremiah, Joel, etc.

We do not need to fast for Christian values, or to become a better Christian; to add the fruit of the Spirit to our lives (Galatians 5:22-23); or to learn how to walk by faith, for such things are the work of the Holy Spirit. The Holy Spirit assists us in applying the attributes of Christianity to our lives, by first giving us the understanding of God's Word, that we may gain the wisdom necessary to live according to the requirements of being the children of God. Although, we may choose to fast to show our heart's sincerity and willingness to submit to the will of God.

> **Philippians 2:12-16** Therefore, my beloved, as you have always obeyed, not as in my presence only, but now much more in my absence, work out your own salvation with fear and trembling; for it is God who works in you both to will and to do for *His* good pleasure. Do all things without complaining and disputing, that you may become blameless and harmless, children of God without fault in the midst of a crooked and perverse generation, among whom you shine as lights in the world, holding fast the word of life, so that I may rejoice in the day of Christ that I have not run in vain or labored in vain.

Many times weaknesses in our lives hinder us from practicing Christian ways. These negative ways intermingle and cause pains in our lives and in those of our loved ones. They manipulate and control (yoke) our lives; these weaknesses can be broken by fasting for one another. People sometimes have a list of weaknesses they believe they are yoked to, but often it is only one or two. It may be difficult to identify a yoke. Many people fail to realize that one yoke may have subsequent effects. For example, anger, bitterness, hatred, and distrust can be the consequences of a yoke of unforgiveness. As the yoke of unforgiveness is broken by fasting, the application of God's Word by the Holy Spirit causes the others to fade away. For example: in modern cars each cylinder has a coil; if one of these coils burns out causing the car to run on one less cylinder, a variety of problems may occur. This loss of power may result in the car starting and or running poorly. Its gas consumption may become excessive and it may become difficult to maintain a high speed. But if the car's difficulties can be pinpointed to the burnt out coil and that coil (often valued as little as $30) is replaced, the other problems will be corrected. When by fasting a yoke of unforgiveness is broken, the by-products of that weakness (anger, distrust, hate, etc.) will fade away.

Once we have been made aware of a weakness we possess, the worse thing we can do is to allow shame to keep it hidden; for when we do, we are giving full power to the enemy to use it against us. "For everyone practicing evil hates the light and does not come to the light, lest his deeds should be exposed. "But he who does the truth comes to the light…" (John 3:20-21). A yoke does not exist that cannot be broken once it is brought to the light, regardless of whether it is a yoke of fear, unforgiveness, selfishness, uncontrolled jealousy, unsubmissiveness (difficulty with or against authority), fault finding, guilt, control (oppressive control of others), anger, shame, rejection, suspicion, etc. Find someone you can trust, someone you know who will be willing to lay down their life for you and fast, and tell them about your weakness. Revealing it is your first step in finding freedom. And as that person fasts for you, you will find deliverance. In turn, a time may present itself when someone confides in you their weakness, and having experienced the liberty that came when someone fasted on your behalf, you can do the same for another. This is how we prove that we are disciples of Jesus and how Christianity (the church) will find victory. The world will know we are Christians by our love.

In addition to the fasting of food for the sake of helping yokes to be broken, the Word speaks of a way that the sincerity of the one fasting can be revealed, adding integrity to the fast. It is neither a command nor a requirement; it is more of a free will offering. A married couple may abstain from physical intimacy, for the time of their fast, revealing their true desire for the freedom of the person they are fasting for, especially if one of the two is fasting for the other. "Do not deprive one another except with consent for a time, that you may give yourselves to fasting and prayer; and come together again so that Satan does not tempt you because of your lack of self-control" (1 Corinthians 7:5). However, fasting physical intimacy should only be added to a fast when both spouses are in agreement to do so.

* * *

HOPE

Hope is a period of time spent waiting, with confidence, for something we have prayed for until we see its manifestation. Hope works together with faith, they cannot be separated; they work together to provide all of our needs. Hope consists of two factors: the first is a *waiting period* and the second is *confidence*.

First: There is the *waiting period* after we pray during which we should not change our confession (prayer).

> **Romans 8:24-25** For we were saved in this hope, but hope that is seen is not hope; for why does one still hope for what he sees? But if we hope for what we do not see, we **eagerly wait** for *it* with perseverance.

Regardless of whether or not we have lifted a prayer on our own behalf or lifted it as an intercessor on behalf of another, there is always a waiting period that follows, a time of hope. It is important, that during this time, we hold on to our confidence knowing that God heard our prayer and, in His perfect time, He will be faithful to answer it. It is during this time that we must become like little children, willing to believe and wait patiently.

> **Matthew 18:3** "Assuredly, I say to you, unless you are converted and become as little children, you will be by no means enter the kingdom of heaven.

> **James 1:3-4** …knowing that the testing of your faith produces patience. But let patience have *its* perfect work, that you may be perfect and complete, lacking nothing.

> **James 5:7** Therefore be patient, brethren, until the coming of the Lord. See *how* the farmer waits for the precious fruit of the earth, waiting patiently for it until it receives the early and latter rain.

Second: We need to maintain a *confidence* that we have and will see what we are believing for.

> **Hebrews 10:35-39,11:1** Therefore do not cast away your **confidence**, which has great reward. For you have need of endurance, so that after you have done the will of God, you may receive the promise: *"For yet a little while, And He who is coming will come and will not tarry. Now the just shall live by faith; But if anyone draws back, My soul has no pleasure in him."* But we are not of those who draw back to perdition, but of those who believe to the saving of the soul. Now faith is the substance of things hoped for, the evidence of things not seen.

Hope is the ability to see "afar off" what you have prayed for knowing that what you are waiting for, will come. The manifestation of your hope may not come instantly, or even in a short time, but it will be faithful to come. We should never cast aside our confidence; it is written that it is God's will to meet our every need, be it for healing, deliverance, protection, wisdom, prosperity, etc. The Lord shows us this in Proverbs 13:12; "Hope deferred makes the heart sick, But *when* the desire comes, *it is* a tree of life." In other words, when our hope (the period of time we spend waiting) seems too long to bear, our heart (our very soul) can grow weary; however, when what we have been hoping for comes to pass, our hearts are revived with joy.

Simply stated, hope is the confidence which helps us to patiently endure the waiting period that follows our petitions. Our faith in God empowers our hope with the confidence we must maintain to withstand the doubts the enemy will generate in our minds. We must not allow those doubts or fears to enter our hearts and cause us to give them utterance.

The recipe for *answered prayers* calls for two important ingredients: the first is faith, and the second is hope. This is what the Lord speaks about in Mark 11.

> **Mark 11:22-24** So Jesus answered and said to them, "Have faith in God. "For assuredly, I say to you, whoever says to this mountain, 'Be removed and be cast into the sea,' and does not doubt in his heart, but believes that those things he says will be done, he will have whatever he says. "**Therefore I say to you, whatever things you ask when you pray, believe that you receive *them*, and you will have *them*.**

The phrase "but believes that those things he says" is referring to the prayers we present to the Lord believing that He hears our requests; this is our faith. And the phrase "and does not doubt in his heart" is referring to the period of time that follows our prayers when we confidently wait to see them fulfilled; this is our hope. The Lord summarized this in the last line of verse 24. Remember Hebrews 11:1, "Now faith is the substance of things hoped for, the evidence of things not seen."

*Faith is to believe God and His Word, to believe
He hears you when you pray and to know that He is faithful
to answer you; it is to believe His promises (His Word)
are forever settled, and that He will not change.*

* * *

*Hope is the waiting period during which you do not
change or repeat your confession (your prayer) and maintain
a confident patience that you have and will see what you
are believing for. Your prayer will be answered.*

CHAPTER FOURTEEN

BEING A DOER

Prayer has great power, especially when it is lifted by one in the presence of another (or others) who are standing in agreement, united by the same faith. Many say, *I have faith, I believe,* but faith must be accompanied by an action, and combined with hope to see its substance. "Thus also faith by itself, if it does not have works, is dead" (James 2:17).

To better help the congregation of my church to grasp the importance of applying an action to our faith, I was led by the Lord to set aside a specific time each week for our church to come together for the purpose of praising Him and lifting prayers. We lift them for one another and for others (those who are not members of our church, even for those who send their petitions from different nations). We call this midweek evening service, *Intercessory Worship.* We begin each service with a testimony of encouragement, followed by the reading of a psalm. The reading is followed by singing praises of exaltation unto the Lord. We spend 20 minutes to an hour praising before the first petition is lifted.

Prayer petitions are written on a large whiteboard, prior to the beginning of and during the service, for all who are gathered to see. As the Holy Spirit moves on the hearts of those in attendance, petitions are lifted. We keep the words of our prayers short, and to the point. We speak the words of the Lord's written Promises over each situation. We are careful to lift only that which someone has requested. When praying publicly, we should not be concerned with impressing others by the words we speak or by how much Scripture we can recite. Prayer is not a forum for glorifying ourselves; it is for our God to be glorified as He meets our needs.

We continue to sing praises of thanksgiving between each petition, knowing that our prayers are being enveloped in our praises, and lifted before the Throne of Grace. This we do together, praising the Lord and interceding on behalf of others until the last petition is lifted. When we learn to combine prayer with the praises of our lips, lifting prayers is no longer a chore, instead it becomes a joy.

We have seen countless prayers answered, prayers for healings from diseases such as cancer and AIDS; for deliverance from addictions; for the restoration of troubled relationships; prayers to be blessed with children, homes, and employment; the list is endless. There is no limit to the Lord's lovingkindness and tender mercies. When we come together for these services to praise, to pray, and to humble ourselves by making our needs or weaknesses known to others, we are putting actions to our faith. These acts would all be in vain if we did not confidently believe that our God faithfully inclines His ears to hear us, and that the desire of His heart is to provide us with all good things. We praise, give thanks (action) and we pray (action). These actions proclaim our faith and give us a hope to stand on.

We close our time of Intercessory Worship with a prayer based on what is written in 1 John 5:14-15; "Now this is the confidence that we have in Him, that if we ask anything according to His will, He hears us. And if we know that He hears us, whatever we ask, we know that we have the petitions that we have asked of Him." We thank the Lord for the confidence He gives us to know that He always hears our petitions. And because we know that He has heard us, we know that our prayers are answered. We ask the Lord to glorify Himself in these things, for He is a good God.

There are many times, as a pastor, I pray alone; I consider each opportunity a privilege and a joy. I have specific worship music that I play during my times of prayer. I try not to enter His presence for the sole purpose of lifting a petition; unless an emergency arises, and even in those situations, I am mindful to worship (acknowledge) Him, to thank Him for His mercies and His faithfulness. I thank Him for all that He provides and for watching over His Word to perform it. It is up to us the church, the body of Christ, to present our God to the world as a loving God. We must come to understand that He *longs* to fellowship with us and that He has countless good thoughts towards us; it is the overwhelming desire of His heart to bless us. In His presence we will find the strength we need to survive our darkest of times. We need to portray Him as One whom we do not need to beg or plead; He always hears us and He cannot help but to be faithful to answer.

CHAPTER FIFTEEN

PRAISE IS THE KEY THAT UNLOCKS OUR CONFIDENCE IN GOD'S WORD

Just as repeating our prayers undermines our confidence in the Word of God, praising the Lord strengthens our confidence in His Word. At one time, it was the cloud of burning incense that was the necessary key that preceded and allowed the blood offering for forgiveness to be presented. Today, the praise of our lips is the key that unlocks Heaven's door, allowing us to present our petitions before the Lord.

> **1 John 5:13-15** These things I have written to you who believe in the name of the Son of God, that you may know that you have eternal life, and that you may *continue to* believe in the name of the Son of God. Now this is the confidence that we have in Him, that if we ask anything according to His will, He hears us. And if we know that He hears us, whatever we ask, we know that we have the petitions that we have asked of Him.

God's Word *is* His will, His testament to us, a love letter; the Bible was written for our wellbeing and it is empowered by the Lord's death. Our prayers are not answered by our works or by repetition; they are answered by our faith that once asked, it is done. God's promises are not *Yes* and *No*, they are *Yes and Amen* (let it be so). "For all the promises of God in Him *are* Yes, and in Him Amen, to the glory of God through us" (2 Corinthians 1:20). The word "amen" is written many times in the Bible. It is used to express: acceptance, agreement, and approval.

When we repeat our prayers, in essence, we are begging. We are reducing the character of the Lord to that of one who *lords* His power over His people. That however, is contrary to the very core of His character.

> **Romans 8:31-32** What then shall we say to these things? If God *is* for us, who *can be* against us? He who did not spare His own Son, but delivered Him up for us all, how shall He not with Him also freely give us all things?

The manner of prayer that most pleases the Lord is the example He Himself set for His disciples in *The Lord's Prayer*. He taught them, when entering into prayer, to first praise. "Our Father in heaven, **Hallowed** be Your name" (Matthew 6:9). The word "hallowed" means: to make holy; purify; consecrate. The Lord wants to be set apart, sanctified, and highly esteemed; He is *worthy*. We should not be like the sons of Aaron who presumptuously entered into God's presence (the Holy of Holies) without wearing the garments required of the high priest. We should instead hallow the Lord by declaring His goodness. He is our Righteousness, our Sanctifier, our Peace, our Provider (Jehovah Jireh), etc.

The names the Lord gave Himself, or allowed Himself to be given, all have specific meanings. His name *Jehovah* expresses, *Keeper of Promises.* When we call Him by the name *Jehovah Jireh*, we are actually declaring that He faithfully promised to provide all of our needs. When we say *Jehovah Rapha*, we are declaring that He faithfully promised to heal us. After Moses encountered the Pharaoh the first time, and witnessed his evilness, he questioned God as to why He had not yet delivered His people. The Lord explained to Moses, that Abraham, Isaac, and Jacob, knew me as God Almighty (*El Shaddai*) but not as *Jehovah* (Promise Keeper) who will be faithful to keep His Word by setting the Israelites free and by bringing them to the Promised Land (Exodus 5:22-23,6:3). The Lord also wanted the meaning of Jehovah (Keeper of Promises) to be remembered by all generations (Exodus 3:15). He is a faithful God; "Jesus Christ *is* the same yesterday, today, and forever" (Hebrews 13: 8).

When we approach the Lord for His help, we should come confidently, acknowledging His faithfulness and His tender mercies; when we acknowledge what He has done for us or for what He is willing to do, we are praising Him. Each time we give thanks for one of His countless provisions, we are recognizing that it is His true nature, His very character, which makes Him so praiseworthy. When we acknowledge Him in song, singing of His greatness, His lovingkindness, His goodness, His longsuffering, and His mercies, we are hallowing His holy name. When we are feeling sad or brokenhearted, or when we are in the middle of a trial, there are songs that bring comfort in the midst of our circumstance. There are also songs that celebrate times of joy and gladness, but whatever the situation, in all the songs we sing, we are proclaiming thanksgiving. Listening to and singing songs of praise assist (help) us with entering into His presence, which provides us with the added bonus of peace of mind and heart. It inspires a confidence in us towards Him and His faithfulness.

CHAPTER SIXTEEN

SWEET FELLOWSHIP

Praising the Lord is a good place to begin a relationship with Him. Praising Him brings answers to prayers and increases our desire to spend devotional time in His presence, comparing our thoughts and actions to His Word. This meditation causes our relationship with the Lord to grow stronger. There is no sweeter fellowship than the times we separate ourselves from the cares of the world to spend quiet moments with the Lord.

> **1 John 1:6-7** If we say that we have fellowship with Him, and walk in darkness, we lie and do not practice the truth. But if we walk in the light as He is in the light, we have fellowship with one another, and the blood of Jesus Christ His Son cleanses us from all sin.

Many of us desire this kind of relationship with the Lord. We want to have the confidence that He hears us and that He is with us always; we want to hear His voice and we want Him to guide us through each day; yet we do not give our time to improve our relationship with Him. The Word encourages us to seek the Lord early; it warns us not to wait until troubles come.

Our "fellowship" is expressed by a *relationship that is based on trust, mutual interests, and open communication.* There is no greater friend (one who puts the needs of another before his own, even unto death) than Jesus. We should start each new day, which in and of itself is a gift from God, with thanksgiving on our lips. Our first thoughts should be of the Lord. We should purpose in our hearts to set aside some time to fellowship with Him; the more time we spend with Him, the more familiar His voice will become. How can we recognize His voice if we are not accustomed to listening for it? We need to seek Him *first* in *all* things. In good times, we need to acknowledge that it is He who is responsible for *every* good thing, and for that we should gratefully thank Him and praise His holy name. In difficult times, we need to acknowledge His tender mercies and His faithfulness to hear our cries and petitions. We should thank Him and praise Him all the more in times of trials because He *never* leaves us or forsakes us; He *diligently* navigates us through every storm.

Faith is the umbrella that enables us, in the
midst of the storm, to sing and dance in the rain.

The Word encourages us to seek the Lord early before the troubles come, and to know troubles *will come.* When we are faithful to seek Him early and to continually praise Him, we too can have the confidence that David expressed in Psalm 18:3, "I will call upon the LORD, *who is worthy* to be praised; So shall I be saved from my enemies." Like Aaron, who was instructed to burn incense twice daily, so that there would be a continual praise offering in readiness for prayers to be presented whenever it was necessary, the Lord also requests the same from us.

Exodus 30:7-9 "Aaron shall burn on it sweet incense every morning; when he tends the lamps, he shall burn incense on it. "And when Aaron lights the lamps at twilight, he shall burn incense on it, a perpetual incense before the LORD throughout your generations. "You shall not offer strange incense on it, or a burnt offering, or a grain offering; nor shall you pour a drink offering on it.

Let us then, constantly (eternally, throughout all time) praise Him. In the same way His readiness to meet our every need never diminishes, neither should our desire to praise Him. We should feel honored that He who is greater than any created being, the Creator of all, desires, even yearns, to have sweet fellowship with us. "The Spirit who dwells in us yearns jealously" (James 4:5b).

It is crucial for our wellbeing to develop a personal relationship with the Lord. It is wise to establish the habit of spending time with the Lord daily. I have encouraged the members of my church to purchase a One Year Bible, being careful to obtain one without commentary; it is very important not to be influenced by the interpretations of man. We should allow only the Holy Spirit and our own pastors, by the Holy Spirit, to give us the understanding of the Word. Each day as we spend time reading and meditating on the Word in our One Year Bible, we are spending time with the Lord, for the Lord is the Word. The more time we spend with the Lord, the more we will come to know Him, and the closer we will come to the realization that we could have no greater friend.

CHAPTER SEVENTEEN

CHANGES ARE RECORDED

Many mistakenly believe that the things that were once required in the Old Testament were only for the time before the cross (the crucifixion of Jesus) and that they were abolished (cancelled, set aside, nullified) after the cross. While that may be the case with some of the Lord's instructions, we should not presume it is the standard for all His instructions. When we are unsure about something, the wise thing to do is to look in the Bible for confirmation. The New Testament *clearly* defines any changes to the requirements that were given in the Old Testament.

Many requirements in the Old Testament were symbolic of things that are required today. Consider what was at one time (before the cross) required as an acceptable sacrifice for the atonement (covering) of sins; it was the sacrifice of a goat, once a year. After the sacrifice of the Lamb of God, those annual sacrifices were no longer required. Jesus paid the price for the salvation of all mankind, a sacrifice so monumental it needed to be paid only once.

Another change the Word clearly describes is when and where the praises of man could be presented to the Lord. Before the cross, the praises of man were presented by one man, the high priest clothed in a special robe with bells on its hem, which gave him safe access behind the veil. There he would burn incense (praise) twice daily. Everyone else remained outside and lifted up their prayers simultaneously. "And the whole multitude of the people was praying outside at the hour of incense" (Luke 1:10). The people would bring certain extracts (spices), to the perfumer who created the crystals that the high priest would then crush into a powder. Some of this crushed incense was stored in the Holy of Holies (Exodus 30:36). The high priest would then sprinkle the incense on the hot coals to create the clouds of incense (praise) before the Lord. Here we see that the people were only indirectly involved in presenting praises unto the Lord:

> **Exodus 25:1-3,6** Then the LORD spoke to Moses, saying: "Speak to the children of Israel, that they may bring Me an offering. From everyone who gives it willingly with his heart you shall take My offering. "And this *is* the offering which you shall take from them: gold, silver, and bronze…oil for the light, and **spices** for the anointing oil and **for the sweet incense**…

Today, the praises of our lips replace the once required clouds of burning incense, allowing those who desire to bring their praises, without any hindrance, into the presence of a living God. There is no longer a veil that separates us from the presence of God. The veil which represented the sins of man was taken away; it was torn in two, at the death of Jesus. "And Jesus cried out with a loud voice, and breathed His last. Then the veil of the temple was torn in two from top to bottom" (Mark 15:37-38). The removal of the veil was a very significant event, for what once separated us (the veil, our sins) from a Holy God no longer remains. The death of Jesus on the cross made us righteous before God and made it possible for ordinary man to enter the presence of God without the fear of death. We can now come directly before Him, into the presence of His holiness, to present our sacrifice of praise as often as we desire. He welcomes us when we sing our way into His presence with words such as these: *We will enter His gates with thanksgiving in our hearts. We will enter His court with praise. We will say this is the day that the Lord has made, we will rejoice for He has made us glad.*

Another clear example of a change, from the Old Testament to the New Testament, can be found written in Matthew 5:27-28, "You have heard that it was said to those of old, '*You shall not commit adultery.*' But I say to you that whoever looks at a woman to lust for her has already committed adultery with her in his heart." At one time the physical act of adultery was sin; today it is sinful when a married person desires (has thoughts, fantasies, plans) about someone other than their spouse.

Many pray, but when they bring their petitions before God, they forget to give thanks (praise). The simplest form of faith, one that greatly pleases the Lord, is to give thanks for what we have not yet seen, but believe we have, because we have asked and it is written. What is written *is* His will. When we give thanks before we lift a petition, knowing that we serve a good God who wants to meet all of our needs, we are displaying an extraordinary faith, an unshakable confidence that we serve a God who always hears and answers.

Praise is essential for our own wellbeing. I know that I shared this earlier, but it is worth repeating. It is vital for our own good, that we like David, understand that as we praise God, not once or twice a week but continually, that God will meet all of our needs and that He will be faithful to deliver us from our enemies as often as the need arises. The best way to thank the Lord for who He is, for what He has done, and for what He continues to do, is to praise Him. Praise Him in all things, from the simplest (a good night's rest) to the greatest (your sick child healed). Praise Him before, in the midst of, and after you have prayed. Praise Him! Praise Him! Praise Him! He will glorify Himself in the midst of our praises. Praise is the key that opens the door allowing us to enter the presence of God; is that not where we all long to be? "But You *are* holy, Enthroned in the praises of Israel" (Psalm 22:3).

> **Psalm 22:1-5** ¹My God, My God, why have You forsaken Me? *Why are You so* far from helping Me, *And from* the words of My groaning? ²O My God, I cry in the daytime, but You do not hear; And in the night season, and am not silent. ³But You *are* holy, Enthroned in the praises of Israel. ⁴Our fathers trusted in You; They trusted, and You delivered them. ⁵They cried to You, and were delivered; They trusted in You, and were not ashamed.

When we examine these Scriptures carefully we will see that verses 1 and 2 were prayer only; in verse 3, praise was added; and in verses 4 and 5, deliverance came.

It was prophesied that there would come a time when Jesus would *sing praises* unto the Father. We can see this confirmed in Psalm 22:22, "I will declare Your name to My brethren; In the midst of the assembly I will praise You." It was written that on the night before the Lord's crucifixion, He offered up praises prior to entering the garden of Gethsemane, before presenting His body as a sacrifice for sins. "And when they had sung **a hymn**, they went out to the Mount of Olives" (Matthew 26:30). The word "hymn" in the preceding verse is translated from the Greek word *humneo*. Its meaning is: to hymn; to sing praises (not just one song or a single hymn). When we look at Acts 16:25, "But at midnight Paul and Silas were praying and **singing hymns** to God," we see the word "hymns" (*humneo*) properly used in its pluralized form. This is also confirmed in Hebrews 2:12, "*I will declare Your name to My brethren; In the midst of the assembly I will **sing praise** to you.*" Jesus sang *praises* unto the Father—not just a single hymn (song). The prophecy was fulfilled; He kept His promise.

We glorify God when we praise Him and He glorifies Himself by answering our prayers. How shall we ever be denied when we ask anything according to His will?

CHAPTER EIGHTEEN

GOD GLORIFIES HIMSELF BY ANSWERING OUR PRAYERS

W hat is *glory*? Is it the setting sun in a blaze of glorious light? Is it the presentation of someone the world perceives as grand or important, someone in a position of authority, displaying their power? Is it the height of personal achievement, such as an Olympian winning a gold medal? Is it the majestic splendor of a king or queen, clothed in their royal robes, crowned with ornate gold, adorned with the finest jewels? Is it the breathtaking beauty of a rainbow that fills the sky after a summer's day rain? We could answer *Yes* to any of the preceding questions and we would be correct; they all represent different types of glory.

However, the grandest glory of all is the glory that is exhibited by a government that truly cares for its people, one that makes providing for their needs its priority. It is displayed by governing with just and impartial laws and it is proven when the governing authorities put the needs of the people before their own. The greatest legacy a nation can pass down to its future generations is not its wealth and military strength alone; it is how it met the needs of its people and their policies to continue to do so.

Consider King Solomon, it is true his God-given gifts of wisdom and knowledge were glorious, as was his palace, his enormous wealth, and his great number of chariots and horses. During her visit with King Solomon, the Queen of Sheba exclaimed:

> **2 Chronicles 9:5b-6** *"It was* a true report which I heard in my own land about your words and your wisdom. "However I did not believe their words until I came and saw with my own eyes; and indeed the half of the greatness of your wisdom was not told me. You exceed the fame of which I heard.

King Solomon's glory did not always extend itself to meeting the needs of his people. Among other things, he built and maintained many temples for the foreign gods of his numerous wives, thus burdening the people with taxation. His governing policies caused the nation to be divided, alienating the Northern tribes after his death. These were certainly not glorious acts of power. You can read more about this in 1 Kings 12.

Whose life demonstrates more glory: a wealthy man who has a fortune in the bank, lives on a grand estate, owns many rare automobiles, and travels to exotic destinations on his private plane or an equally wealthy man, who lives in a modest home, owns a decent automobile, and instead of spending his money on private jets and exotic getaways, uses his finances to improve the lives of those less fortunate who live in his community? The glory of the man who shares his wealth, by providing for the needs of others, is greatly magnified as those who benefit from it speak of his goodness, glorifying his name.

Christianity (the church) can be thought of as a nation, governed by Almighty God, who displays the glory of His goodness as He faithfully meets the needs of all the people. God governs by the most just and impartial laws of all; those written in the Bible. Jesus was sent to reveal God's majesty, His splendor, and His power of creation. But foremost, He was sent by His Father to reveal the glory of God, the fullness of His immeasurable goodness to His people and to the world. This was confirmed by Christ Himself, just before He departed from His disciples and spoke to His Father. "I have glorified You on the earth. I have finished the work which You have given Me to do" (John 17:4). His work was to show the goodness of God, His willingness to meet all of our needs. Jesus was sent to reveal His Father's love for the world (for all) which was culminated at the cross for our redemption, restoration, and healing. He gave His life as the physical expression of that love.

Let us examine John 9:3-4, "Jesus answered, 'Neither this man nor his parents sinned, but that the works of God should be revealed in him. "I must work the works of Him who sent Me while it is day; *the* night is coming when no one can work." Here we see Jesus explaining that restoring sight to the man who was blind since birth, was simply an act of obedience (work) to the Father. It was through these acts that the goodness of God was evidenced on the earth. The glory of God's goodness was also demonstrated when Jesus restored a lifeless Lazarus, who was the breadwinner of his family. The Lord spared Martha and Mary from having to depend on the townspeople to meet their needs; essentially, they were delivered from living as beggars. Jesus said to her, "Did I not say to you that if you would believe you would see the glory of God?" (John 11:40). See a similar example of God's goodness in Luke 7:12-15.

In the following verses, Jesus declares that whatever we ask in His name, He will perform so that the Father's goodness (glory) will be revealed:

> **John 14:13-14** "And whatever you ask in My name, that I will do, **that the Father may be glorified** in the Son. "If you ask anything in My name, I will do *it*."

> **John 15:7-8** "If you abide in Me, and My words abide in you, you will ask what you desire, and it shall be done for you. "**By this My Father is glorified**, that you bear much fruit; so you will be My disciples."

> *Faith takes courage. Jesus promised that He would answer the prayers of anyone brave enough to believe, showing them the goodness of their Heavenly Father.*

The Father glorifies Himself by meeting *all* of our needs; each time He answers a prayer He is declaring His goodness. He is showing us the abundant riches of His goodness, His beauty, His splendor, His majesty, His excellence, His greatness, i.e. His glory. His grace and tender mercies prove that. God revealed these attributes to Moses in the following:

> **Exodus 33:18-19** And he said, "Please, show me Your glory." Then He said, "I will make **all My goodness** pass before you, and I will proclaim the name of the LORD before you. I will be gracious to whom I will be gracious, and I will have compassion on whom I will have compassion."

Exodus 34:6-7 And the LORD passed before him and proclaimed, "The LORD, the LORD God, merciful and gracious, longsuffering, and abounding in goodness and truth, "keeping mercy for thousands, forgiving iniquity and transgression and sin…

God revealed His goodness (His glory) to Moses; however, Moses failed to show the goodness of God to the people. He did not reveal the *willingness* of the Lord to meet their needs. As their shepherd, above all other things, it was his responsibility to convey through his communications with the people, that the Lord was a good and loving God. Instead, Moses by his actions represented/portrayed the Lord as an angry, harsh God. As a result, the Lord did not allow Moses to bring the people into the good land that flowed with milk and honey, the land which revealed the goodness and the *willingness* of God to provide the peoples needs. This, God did Himself; God glorified Himself.

Numbers 20:7-12 Then the LORD spoke to Moses, saying, "Take the rod; you and your brother Aaron gather the congregation together. Speak to the rock before their eyes, and it will yield its water; thus you shall bring water for them out of the rock, and give drink to the congregation and their animals." So Moses took the rod from before the LORD as He commanded him. And Moses and Aaron gathered the assembly together before the rock; and he said to them, "Hear now, you rebels! Must we bring water for you out of this rock?" Then Moses lifted his hand and stuck the rock twice with his rod; and water came out abundantly, and the congregation and their animals drank. Then the LORD spoke to

Moses and Aaron, **"Because you did not believe Me, to hallow Me in the eyes of the children of Israel, therefore you shall not bring this assembly into the land which I have given them."**

There are many places in the Bible where it is written, "You shall see the glory of the Lord"; "Great is the glory of the Lord"; "The glory of the Lord shall be revealed." These statements are often followed by the Lord telling His people you will see My goodness; you will see your prayers answered; you will see deliverance and restoration; and you will see your needs provided and My promises fulfilled.

Jesus' very life was praise unto the Father; the Father told Him, "I will glorify Myself in You." In other words, the Father told His Son, *In You I will reveal My goodness, My salvation and full restoration to all who call on My name.* This is confirmed in John 13:31-32, "So, when he had gone out, Jesus said, 'Now the Son of Man is glorified, and God is glorified in Him. If God is glorified in Him, God will also glorify Him in Himself, and glorify Him immediately.'"

In Isaiah 60, in the last part of verse 7, the Lord says, "I will glorify the house of My glory." The word "house" is referring to us, both individually and collectively as a church. When we praise Him He is glorified, and so will we also be glorified (saved by Him; our needs, whatever they may be, met by Him). "Whoever offers praise glorifies Me; And to him who orders *his* conduct *aright* I will show the salvation of God" (Psalm 50:23).

We glorify the Lord when we bestow upon Him adoration, praise, and thanksgiving. As we hallow His name, by singing songs of exaltation that describe His worthiness, we are glorifying Him. As we praise God, He magnifies His presence. What greater way is there for us to acknowledge God and His presence than by giving thanks (praises) for whom He is, and for all He has done, and continues to do. We thank Him because of our confidence in Him and His faithfulness to watch over His Word to perform it.

God wants to glorify Himself in us; He
wants to reveal His goodness to the world through
us by our lifestyles and by the love we show.

CHAPTER NINETEEN

THE LORD'S PASSION TO ESTABLISH HIS CHURCH

Jerusalem/Zion is symbolic of the church. In His Word the Lord asks us to hold Him accountable to His promise to establish Jerusalem (the church) as "a praise in the earth." He asks us to remind Him of His promises, not for His benefit, because He is neither forgetful nor unfaithful. He asks for *our* benefit, so that we will practice both to use, and stand on His Word.

> **Isaiah 62:1,6-7** For Zion's sake I will not hold My peace, And for Jerusalem's sake I will not rest, Until her righteousness goes forth as brightness, And her salvation as a lamp *that* burns. I have set watchman on your walls, O Jerusalem; They shall never hold their peace day or night. You who make mention of the LORD, do not keep silent, And give Him no rest till He establishes And till He makes Jerusalem a praise in the earth.

In the Book of Daniel, the Lord told Daniel that He would reveal to him the Scriptures that would detail how He would deliver and return Israel, after seventy years of slavery, and also things to come in the future. He told Daniel that no one upholds Him (holds Him accountable to His Word). By believing and trusting Him to keep His Word, we give Him strength. The enemy withstands us from receiving the understanding of God's Word. For when we come to know of His blessings, we can through praise, prayers, and fasting, press in and claim them as our own. It is the violent who take hold of them by force.

> **Daniel 10:12-14,21** Then he said to me, "Do not fear, Daniel, for from the first day that you set your heart to understand, and to humble yourself before your God, your words were heard; and I have come because of your words. "But the prince of the kingdom of Persia withstood me twenty-one days; and behold, Michael, one of the chief princes, came to help me, for I had been left alone there with the kings of Persia. "Now I have come to make you understand what will happen to your people in the latter days, for the vision *refers* to *many* days yet *to come*." "But I will tell you what is noted in the Scripture of Truth. (No one upholds me against these, except Michael your prince.

He Keeps His Promises: Since the time of His introduction to the Israelites, as the Lord Jehovah, the Keeper of Promises, the Lord has demonstrated His power. An example of that power was revealed when He brought great plagues down on the Egyptians, delivering the Israelites from slavery, with not one among them sick or poor as they made their great exodus from Egypt. Until the time they stood on the shores of the Red Sea, the Lord provided their every need without having to be asked, for all He provided, was based on His promise to Abraham and His faithfulness to keep His Word. But as the Egyptians drew near, the Israelites fearing for their safety and freedom, cried out to God:

> **Exodus 14:15-16** And the LORD said to Moses, "Why do you cry to Me? Tell the children of Israel to go forward. "But lift up your rod, and stretch out your hand over the sea and divide it. And the children of Israel shall go on dry *ground* through the midst of the sea.

The rod the Lord spoke of in the preceding Scriptures was symbolic of His Word. He was asking Moses to hold Him to His Word. He not only promised to deliver the Israelites from their oppressors, He also promised to bring them to the Promised Land. God wanted to be held accountable to His Word. He was teaching His people that He would be faithful to His Word; He wanted them to stand on the Word with a bold confidence.

Many years later, God prophesied through Isaiah (Isaiah 62:1,6-7) His desire to establish His people. He also prophesied through Daniel, in Daniel 10:21b, "No one upholds Me against these, except Michael your prince." The same trust that was required of the Israelites, as they stood on the shores of the Red Sea, while their oppressors drew near (Exodus 10:13), is required of us today. The Lord encourages the church (us) to do the same (to put our trust in Him), no matter what trial or storm the enemy brings. The enemy will be relentless in his attempts to blind us from seeing the truth about God's goodness and will cause us to block our blessings. We need to stand firmly on the promises of God and know that He will be faithful to watch over His Word to fulfill it.

The Lord said to come boldly to His Throne of Grace; to take hold of, and receive His mercy, finding grace to help us in times of need (Hebrews 4:16). We need boldness to enter the presence of God. We also need a willingness to humbly acknowledge our wrongs. Acknowledging them is the first step to turning from them. Do not allow your wrongdoings to stop you from entering in. The mercies of God, His goodness, and faithfulness towards us have nothing to do with what we have or have not done or with what we do or do not deserve; they are based on His unconditional love for us. It is in His presence that we can find the strength to change our sinful ways. We must, as David did, come to understand this. The tax collector (in Luke 18) did not allow his sins to stop him from entering the Lord's presence to ask for forgiveness, in spite of how unworthy he felt.

Praise does not wash away our sins; it may however make us aware of them so that we can ask for forgiveness. David praised his way to victory, receiving answers to prayers. He was a faithful praise and worshiper; praise kept him in the presence of the Lord. When the bear and the lion challenged him, God's anointing gave David the strength to slay them. This was also the case when he slew Goliath. We too are able to defeat the deceitful enemy. There are many places in the Bible where the Word declares that praising the Lord gives us victory over our enemies. Paul and Silas, beaten and imprisoned, praised the Lord. Their praise in the midst of their circumstances caused their cells to be opened and their shackles to be loosed. All who were there heard but did not participate. Was it their silence that cost them their freedom?

When we learn to praise and worship God, before lifting
a prayer petition to Him, we will have more confidence and
we will see more, if not all, of our prayers answered.

CHAPTER TWENTY

PRAISE HIM
ACCEPT YOUR FREEDOM

It has been more than 2000 years since Jesus went to the cross and paid the price for our freedom. Why is it then that so many Christians remain in bondage to weaknesses, even though their prison doors have been opened and their shackles loosed? There has never been, and there will never again be, as great a gift as the one the world received when, in His perfect innocence, Christ paid the ultimate price for all. But to benefit from so great a gift, we must first come to understand that it is through praising Him that we will find the freedom He provided when He laid His life down.

We see so many at church and at Christian conventions, who do not open their mouths to sing praises. Some sit during praise and worship; some stay away altogether, they remain outside waiting for praise and worship to end before entering. Some hold back their praises because they believe they do not have good singing voices. Some offer reserved praises because they have been made to feel inferior for other reasons. Sadly, so many have not come to the realization that we praise God to enter His presence, to receive the freedom He has provided, and for the strength needed for our daily lives.

We should not allow the devil, another person, or even our own insecurities or weaknesses to keep us from our freedom. PRAISE HIM! PRAISE HIM! PRAISE HIM! He asks us repeatedly in the psalms to make a joyful noise. We have seen it written, in the opening of the Bible, that the Lord requires us to mix our prayers with praises (incense). In the closing book of the Bible, the Lord personally requests the same:

> **Revelation 4:8-11** *The* four living creatures, each having six wings, were full of eyes around and within. And they do not rest day or night, saying: "Holy, holy, holy, Lord God Almighty, Who was and is and is to come!" Whenever the living creatures give glory and honor and thanks to Him who sits on the throne, who lives forever and ever, the twenty-four elders fall down before Him who sits on the throne and worship Him who lives forever and ever, and cast their crowns before the throne, saying: "You are worthy, O Lord, To receive glory and honor and power; For You created all things, And by Your will they exist and were created."

The following verse describes incense, already combined with the prayers of the saints, being offered before the Lord:

> **Revelation 5:8** Now when He had taken the scroll, the four living creatures and the twenty-four elders fell down before the Lamb, each having a harp, and golden bowls full of incense, which are the prayers of the saints.

Prayers are not praise (incense), they are petitions. Praise is the fruit of our lips. David's declaration was made while he was praising the Lord, "Let my prayer be set before You *as* incense, The lifting up of my hands *as* the evening sacrifice" (Psalm 141:2). David understood that troubles would come, time and time again, and that he would continually need deliverance; so he learned to be a *praise warrior.* God taught David to be a warrior. But no warrior, no matter how great, will be successful if he or she does not know to praise the Lord God Almighty in the midst of their battles. As David praised God, not allowing the trials brought by the enemy to hinder him, God was glorified and the glory of God brought light to David's darkest moments. He enveloped his prayers in praise (the psalms) and knew no matter what the situation, he would live to praise God.

Give this simple illustration some thought: Milk has a plain taste, but when we add sugar and a few other simple ingredients and mix them all together, we have ice cream. The plain tasting milk no longer tastes plain. It has become sweet to the taste. When we mix prayer with praise, it becomes like sweet incense in God's presence.

As the twenty-four elders continued to praise God, enveloping the prayers of the saints in praise, their praise assisted the prayers in ascending before the Lord; even the angels joined in to praise the Lord:

> **Revelation 5:9-14** And they sang a new song, saying: "You are worthy to take the scroll, And to open its seals; For You were slain, And have redeemed us to God by Your blood Out of every tribe and tongue and people and nation, And have made us kings and priests to our God; And we shall reign on the earth." Then I looked, and I heard the voice of many angels

around the throne, the living creatures, and the elders; and the number of them was ten thousand times ten thousand, and thousands of thousands, saying with a loud voice: "Worthy is the Lamb who was slain To receive power and riches and wisdom, And strength and honor and glory and blessing!" And every creature which is in heaven and on the earth and under the earth and such as are in the sea, and all that are in them, I heard saying: "Blessing and honor and glory and power *Be* to Him who sits on the throne, And to the Lamb, forever and ever!" Then the four living creatures said, "Amen!" And the twenty-four elders fell down and worshiped Him who lives forever and ever.

In Revelation 8, we see it written that an angel stood at the altar of incense in Heaven, with a golden censer to receive incense to combine with all the prayers of the saints, that they may ascend before God. Once again, this is showing us that it is our praise that carries our prayers before God.

Revelation 8:3-4 Then another angel, having a golden censer, came and stood at the altar. He was given much incense, that he should offer *it* with the prayers of all the saints upon the golden altar which was before the throne. And the smoke of the incense, with the prayers of the saints, ascended before God from the angel's hand.

Angels Long to Praise with Us: The true praises of our lips are the most highly regarded in Heaven; they are above all other praises in all of God's creation, in Heaven, and on Earth.

(I believe that is the reason that the angels long to join us in our praises of the Lord.) It is written that angels were created to sing praises around the throne of God. It is their greatest joy to join in with the praises of the saints here on Earth, when we are praising and worshiping God.

> **Psalm 148:1-2** PRAISE the LORD! Praise the LORD from the heavens; Praise Him in the heights! Praise Him, all His angels; Praise Him, all His hosts!

> **Hebrews 1:6** But when He again brings the first-born into the world, He says:*"Let all the angels of God worship Him."*

> **Revelation 5:11-12** Then I looked, and I heard the voice of many angels around the throne, the living creatures, and the elders; and the number of them was ten thousand times ten thousand, and thousands of thousands, saying with a loud voice: "Worthy is the Lamb who was slain To receive power and riches and wisdom, And strength and honor and glory and blessing!"

Many people claim that they have actually heard angels singing along with them in church. Some have even had their eyes opened to see Heaven's angels praising God in their midst. While we are praising the Lord, the room fills with angels who are watching over us before we lift prayer petitions to Him. They are listening, waiting, and desiring an opportunity to praise God along with us. Because of their (angels) presence while we are praising and worshiping the Lord, we are blessed with the extra bonus of knowing that they were sent by God to serve us and they stand ready to carry out our requests (example: traveling mercies, hedge of protection, etc.).

> **Psalm 91:10-12** No evil shall befall you, Nor shall any plague come near your dwelling; For He shall give His angels charge over you, To keep you in all your ways. In *their* hands they shall bear you up, Lest you dash your foot against a stone.

CHAPTER TWENTY-ONE

FREED FROM GLOOM

Many of the battles we fight against the enemy take place in the battlefields of our minds, as Satan manipulates our thoughts and then uses them against us. The enemy oppresses us with thoughts of doom and gloom. Many people suffer from mood swings and varying degrees of depression, which often leads to thoughts of suicide. Periods of depression can be brought on by listening to gossip or accepting negative thoughts. These are all works of the enemy.

We often seek others to petition God on our behalf when we need deliverance from the attacks of depression, and God delivers us. The enemy however, is relentless. He will return at a more opportune time and will attempt to rob us of our peace, time and time again; he has nothing to lose and our souls to gain.

> **2 Corinthians 10:4-5** For the weapons of our warfare *are* not carnal but mighty in God for pulling down strongholds, casting down arguments and every high thing that exalts itself against the knowl-

edge of God, bringing every thought into captivity to the obedience of Christ...

We must learn to defend ourselves against the attacks of depression the enemy brings, without having to continually ask others to pray for us. When we arm ourselves with the Word of God, knowing that we are never truly alone, believing that when we call on the name of Jesus, He is there to help us do battle, we will always be victorious. "Therefore submit to God. Resist the devil and He **will** flee from you" (James 4:7). Being obedient to the Word of God, remaining confident that He always hears us and that He will be faithful to deliver us, and singing praises of adoration and thanksgiving to His name are our best defense.

The best way to silence the negative thoughts the enemy bombards our minds with is to praise our God. Praising God *is the best* weapon to use against the evil works of Satan. When we learn to praise God in the midst of our troubles the enemy will flee from us.

> **1 Samuel 16:23** And so it was, whenever the spirit from God was upon Saul, that David would take a harp and play *it* with his hand. Then Saul would become refreshed and well, and the **distressing spirit** would depart from him.

This verse speaks of a time when the Spirit of the Lord departed from Saul because he disobeyed a commandment of the Lord. And because of his disobedience, a distressing spirit would trouble (oppress) him. Saul's servants, seeing his torment, beseeched their master to send them out to find a man who was a skillful player of the harp.

1 Samuel 16:16-18 "Let our master now command your servants, *who are* before you, to seek out a man *who is* a skillful player on the harp. And it shall be that he will play it with his hand when the distressing spirit from God is upon you, and you shall be well." So Saul said to his servants, "Provide me now a man who can play well, and bring *him* to me." Then one of the servants answered and said, "Look, I have seen a son of Jesse the Bethlehemite, *who is* skillful in playing, a mighty man of valor, a man of war, prudent in speech, and a handsome person; and the LORD *is* with him."

Saul sent for David. It was when David played his harp, in praise of the Lord, that the distressing spirit would depart from Saul and he would find relief, become refreshed and well, and find freedom from depression.

Throughout the Bible there are stories about the enemy's attacks on God's people and how when the people began praising God during their battles their enemies would be scattered. This is based on God's promise to us in Deuteronomy 28:7, "The LORD will cause your enemies who rise against you to be defeated before your face; they shall come out against you one way and flee before you seven ways."

Philippians 4:4-7 Rejoice in the Lord always. Again I will say, rejoice! Let your gentleness be known to all men. The Lord *is* at hand. Be anxious for nothing, but in everything by prayer and supplication, with thanksgiving, let your requests be made known to God; and the peace of God, which

surpasses all understanding, will guard your hearts
and minds through Christ Jesus.

When we submit to the will of the enemy by allowing him to
rule over our flesh, our minds, and emotions (feelings) with wor-
ries, anxieties, doubts, fears, suspicions, bitterness, boredom or
even with *poor me* attitudes, we will be unable to live as Philippians 4:4a declares, "Rejoice in the Lord always." The word "rejoice"
means: to be joyful, cheerful, calmly happy, be glad, rejoice. It is
very difficult to rejoice when we are burdened by the weight of the
negative emotions that the enemy brings. These emotional burdens often affect our physical wellbeing (headaches, high blood
pressure, insomnia, heart problems) as well as our physical appearance (frown lines, hair loss, weight gain/loss). In some cases, those
suffering from extreme oppression/depression may even develop
hunched backs, as the daughter of Abraham (Luke 13:11-16). Philippians 4:5a states, "Let your gentleness be known to all men." It is
only when we do not allow anxiety to overtake us, knowing that
the Lord is present to help, not forgetting, "if God is for us, who
can be against us," will we be able to exude a spirit of gentleness.

The aforementioned negatives rob us from our ability to be
gentle with others. Many times we become harsh, irritable, and
impatient with those who are in need of our help or assistance.
When we are abrupt/short with others, it becomes evident that
the enemy has robbed us of our peace. As soon as we come to the
realization that we have lost our peace we should begin praising
the Lord. This will change what the enemy meant for wrong into
an opportunity to take hold of the peace of God and by that peace,
we will be able to apologize and extend our help to those in need.

Praise God continually. Praise Him before you pray, as you
pray, and after you have prayed, so regardless of when the enemy
comes with his attempts to oppress you, your praises will deliver

you. This will cause the enemy to flee and it will give you rest/ peace of mind; it will also strengthen your confidence in your Christian walk. When we learn to walk in the Spirit the enemy will be unable to force his will on us, and "...the peace of God, which surpasses all understanding, will guard your hearts and minds." We will then be able to help others whom the enemy oppresses, to do the same. There are many who have been in the body of Christ for years (including church leaders) that are attacked and oppressed by the enemy.

I would like to share a personal testimony, one I hope will encourage those of you who have not yet grasped that the surest way to resist the enemy is by praising the Lord.

> Whenever my wife, Stella, finds herself in a difficult situation she plays praise and worship music. She spends serious time praising and worshiping the Lord. She thanks Him for all good things; she continually blesses His Holy name. This brings peace to her mind; she is then able to resist the enemy, causing him to flee from her. With her new found peace of mind, she remains the same sweet person she was before the enemy's attacks on her mind. She is able to justify and forgive the person(s) the enemy was using to attack her. I have learned much about praising the Lord, in the midst of my trials, from the example she sets before me.

Do Not Replace the Veil: There is no longer a veil that separates us from the Throne of Grace (the presence of God). The veil (the sins of our flesh) that once prevented us from entering into the presence of a Holy God was removed, as our sins were removed (forgiven, paid in full), at the cross. Now, freed from the debt of our sins, we can freely enter the presence of God without any hindrance, and present the sacrifice of praise ourselves. The burning smoke of incense is no longer required; today, it is the live praises of our lips that the Lord desires.

> **Leviticus 16:13-14** "And he shall put the incense on the fire before the LORD, that the cloud of incense may cover the mercy seat that *is* on the Testimony, lest he die." He shall take some of the blood of the bull and sprinkle *it* with his finger on the mercy seat on the east *side;* and before the mercy seat he shall sprinkle some of the blood with his finger seven times.

We see in the preceding verses, as we saw earlier, that covering the mercy seat with the cloud of incense was required by the Lord before the petitions were presented. We also see in the first chapter of Luke, that this practice continued while prayers were presented and answered. It is in the midst of our praises that our prayers are answered and that miracles take place.

> **Luke 1:8-17** So it was, that while he was serving as priest before God in the order of his division, according to the custom of the priesthood, his lot fell to burn incense when he went into the temple of the Lord. **And the whole multitude of people was praying outside at the hour of incense.** Then an angel of the Lord appeared to him, standing on the right side of the altar of incense. And when Zacharias saw *him,* he was troubled, and fear fell upon him. But the angel said to him, "Do not be afraid,

Zacharias, for your prayer is heard; and your wife Elizabeth will bear you a son, and you shall call his name John. "And you will have joy and gladness, and many will rejoice at his birth. "For he will be great in the sight of the Lord, and shall drink neither wine nor strong drink. He will also be filled with the Holy Spirit, even from his mother's womb. "And he will turn many of the children of Israel to the Lord their God. "He will also go before Him in the spirit and power of Elijah, '*to turn the hearts of the fathers to the children,*' and the disobedient to the wisdom of the just, to make ready a people prepared for the Lord."

Zacharias, the high priest, and his wife, longed for a child and petitioned God; it was when Zacharias was offering up incense (praise) that his request was answered. We also see in these same verses, that the people prayed at the moment the incense was burning, understanding that they needed to present their petitions at a time when their prayers could ascend before God in the cloud of smoke. Zacharias and his wife were blessed with a son, not an ordinary son, but the forerunner (John the Baptist), the one sent to prepare the way for the Messiah. And the people received the answer to their prayers; their petition for a Messiah was answered; they received a Savior, Jesus, not for Israel alone but for the world as well.

We must be careful not to allow the enemy to separate us from the Lord, with doubts or fears, causing us to replace the veil that was once torn away. We need to maintain the confidence that we can, at any time, boldly approach the Throne of Grace. We need to faithfully attend church, so that we can be nourished by the very Word (armor of God) that strengthens and protects us, as we apply it to our lives. We need to continually praise the Lord, spending time in His presence so that we may become accustomed to the sound of His voice. Jesus went to the cross to be Savior for all; but for us, who believe and have accepted Him into our hearts, He is Lord. Do not allow any devil to separate you from Him.

CHAPTER TWENTY-TWO

THE POWER OF THE PRESENTATION

As we established earlier, incense is symbolic of praise and the Lord requires the sacrifice of our praise (incense) before we lift our petitions up to Him. We also learned that the Lord wants us to pray boldly and straightforwardly; most importantly, He does not want us to repeat our prayers, as that is displaying a lack of faith that He always hears us. When, by the guidance of the Holy Spirit, I grasped the significance of these revelations, I began sharing them with the body of Christ.

I started with those who were close at hand, my church, Covenant Temple. Next, in obedience to the Lord, I answered His call by writing about these revelations in my first edition of *Worship the Lord in Prayer*. While I was working on that book, I was inspired by the Holy Spirit to create the *Incense Is Symbolic of Praise* presentation to better help illustrate the Lord's message. And now in this expounded version of *Worship the Lord in Prayer*, I am able to share the impact that sharing these revelations through the presentation has had on the lives of others.

To enhance the presentation and to make it as realistic as possible, we designed and produced a simple version of the robe worn by the high priest. **See the illustration to the right**. Paying special attention to the hem of the garment, we attached alternating bells of gold (gold plated brass bells) and artificial pomegranates to its circumference. During the presentations, while wearing the robe, I burned incense on a basic example of the altar of incense. As the cloud of incense ascended and filled the room, those in attendance began to grasp the purpose of the demonstration; and the importance

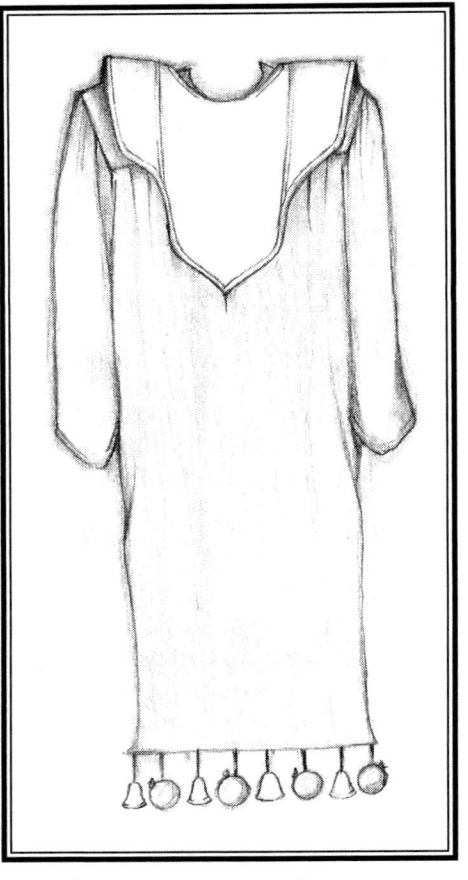

of, and power that comes through combining praise with prayer.

We have demonstrated this presentation to various groups of churches in different nations. Using this visual display helped many understand the biblical symbols and their purposes, and made it easier for them to take hold of the importance and the power of praise. We have been overwhelmed by the responses we have witnessed. We presented it for the first time at a convention in Atlanta, Georgia; there were over two thousand in attendance. People, who in the past were encumbered by hindrances, began praising God. More than once the leaders of the convention tried to stop the people from praising and worshiping so that they could continue the conference, but their attempts to silence the worshipers only caused them to praise louder; some began falling out in the Spirit. When those in charge finally got the people to stop praising the Lord, the convention's organizer declared, *We have just witnessed a touch of Heaven.*

I heard the Lord speak to me at that moment, saying, *Wherever this presentation is given and received, I will give a touch of revival.* The Lord has been faithful to His promise; after seeing the presentation, some churches praised God for hours. We witnessed pastors falling out in the Spirit and saying afterwards they never felt such a strong anointing. Churches that had let praise and worship be overshadowed by other things brought it back to the forefront, bringing glory to God and freedom to those who were once intimidated by praise. Wherever we travel with this message, we see the Lord bringing new life to prayer, fulfilling His Word and performing miracles.

The following are the eyewitness testimonies of Jason Martucci. He joined the church as a young man and has since been raised up to the position of an elder. He has a servant's heart and I am blessed by his willingness to support my work both at home and in the mission field. It has been a privilege to have had him accompany me to present the Incense Is Symbolic of Praise presentation.

* * *

~ Atlanta, Georgia ~

In August of 2000, filled with hope and anticipation, I accompanied my Pastor, to Atlanta, Georgia, where he was invited to speak at a convention. I went to support his work and to witness the incense presentation for the first time on the road. He was invited by the convention's organizer after she witnessed the presentation at our church. She was so touched by it that she asked him to present it at the convention later that year. Pastor John was scheduled to speak on the second night of the week long event; this was to allow for any latecomers to be in attendance. After witnessing the praise and worship sessions that had taken place on the first day, I remember feeling first angry and then grieved that only about twenty-five percent of those in attendance seemed to be genuinely praising the Lord. The others were openly socializing, laughing, and walking about. I was initially angry because I felt that those who were not praising the Lord were being disrespectful of His majesty, but my anger soon changed to sorrow because I came to realize that these people simply did not understand the Lord's worthiness to be praised.

That night I prayed, asking the Lord to prepare the hearts of His people to receive the important message, that by the Holy Spirit, my pastor would be presenting. I was concerned because he was allotted only twenty minutes to deliver the message. But knowing that with God all things are possible, I went to sleep with a hope in my heart. In those short but Holy Spirit filled minutes, ears were opened to hear and hearts were moved to receive the understanding that praise is the key which opens the door to the presence of God. I never could have imagined what I witnessed when he, like the high priest in the days of old, sprinkled the incense over the hot coals. It was truly one of the most amazing things I have ever seen. Almost simultaneously, the nearly three thousand people in attendance lifted their hands and spontaneously broke out praising and worshiping the Lord. What I witnessed greatly differed from what I had seen the day before. Some were so caught up in their worship that they were hanging over the upper level balcony.

The door was opened wide and the people continued to praise for a long, long time. When the praises began to wane, a pianist began playing and once again the room swelled with the sounds of adoration and thanksgiving for the Lord. Soon there were trumpets sounding, and the blowing of shofars (ram's horns). And, a replica of the ark of the covenant was carried out onto the stage. It took the convention's organizers quite some time to silence the people so that the program could continue. Miracles took place in that room as God touched His people.

* * *

~ Africa ~

During one of our earliest trips to Africa, we visited a church in Tema, Ghana. Shortly after completing the incense presentation we had to leave, because we were expected at another church. We were later told that the church in Tema continued to praise the Lord after we had left, and a blind man in the rear of the church began to cry out, *I can see! I can see!* In response to hearing his claim, the pastor called to him and said, *If you can see, come to me.* The newly sighted man walked through the people until he stood before the pastor. The pastor challenged him again and said, *If you can still see, return to your seat.* And so he did. In the midst of the praises, God not only opened hearts to receive but He also opened eyes to see; His glory was revealed to all those gathered there that day.

One of my most vivid recollections is of the time we traveled to Nigeria to present the *Worship the Lord in Prayer* message. The year was 2004 and Pastor John was invited by the Harp and Bowl Ministry, to speak at a conference they were hosting. He accepted the invitation, but just prior to traveling to Nigeria, a time of unrest and striking broke out and there was a great concern that rioting would follow. He was asked if he would like to withdraw his acceptance; he declined saying, *We gave our word and we know that God will watch over us.*

We arrived to find that two of the other guest speakers from the United States, one an evangelist, the other a Nigerian pastor whose church was in the States, had cancelled their trips. The host ministry invited a locally well-known minister to speak to help fill the gap left by those who had cancelled. Pastor John was visibly upset by what that minister was preaching to the people gathered there. He spoke words of condemnation that were both unedifying and offensive. He told the people that their heritage was one of witchcraft and that they should not lose sight of the fact that they were descendants of witches and warlocks.

Disheartened by what he had just heard, when it was his turn to speak, by the Holy Spirit, Pastor John boldly declared, *Those of you who have accepted Jesus have been released from paying the price for the sins of your parents. That price was paid on the cross, with His precious blood.* At that moment, his hand slammed down on the glass podium. It sounded as if it had been struck by a bolt of lightning. The impact caused the glass podium to split vertically into seven pieces, all of which remained upright in their base. In response to his offer to pay to have the podium replaced, Pastor John was told, *No, we have just been blessed to see the hand of God deliver us (break the back) from a curse.* Though the ministry replaced it, they left the fractured one on display for the remainder of the conference as a witness of what they had heard and experienced.

In 2008, we were invited a fourth time to Africa. This time it was a Presbyterian pastor (he was also a district overseer in Ghana), who had been given a copy of *Worship the Lord in Prayer* by a colleague of Pastor John's. After reading the book, he invited Pastor John to share its message with the church. The invitation was initially met with some reservation; however, in spite of the reservation, the invitation was not withdrawn, thus allowing the pastors and leaders to come and hear what the Holy Spirit had to say.

When he finished preaching, he presented the incense presentation. It was awesome to see the people grasp a new understanding, a new purpose, for praising Jesus. One pastor, whose nature was to be very dignified and reserved, began jumping up and down. The congregation, hungry to know more about the power and freedom that comes when praise is combined with prayers, literally stampeded towards the table where the books, *Worship the Lord in Prayer*, were being displayed, fearful that there would not be enough to go around.

* * *

~ The Philippines ~

In the summer of 2007, we were invited to preach at a Pastors and Leaders Conference in the province of Tabuk, in Northern Luzon, Philippines. Approximately three hundred pastors and leaders from Kalinga (a rural mountain region) attended. Once again I was overwhelmed by what I witnessed.

Pastor John shared the message *Worship the Lord in Prayer* combined with teachings on praise and worship; he also presented the incense presentation. These once extremely reserved people began to sing and dance. Their shackles of restraint were broken and replaced with joy and freedom as they were enraptured in worship. They would not be silenced. The host pastor was so moved by what he had just witnessed, he asked Pastor John if he would share the message with his church before leaving the Philippines. Pastor John accepted his invitation.

Before I go on, it is important to understand, that this pastor's church had absolutely no praise or music as part of its services. We were surprised and elated when we arrived to find drums and other instruments in the church just days after the pastor and leaders had witnessed the presentation. And in only a few days time, they were singing and playing modern songs of praise.

* * *

~ South America ~

In 2008, we also traveled to South America for the first time. We visited Berbice, Guyana, where Pastor John spoke at a Pastors and Leaders Conference. While there he also presented the incense presentation, during which a demon-possessed woman walked in off the street and received a complete healing. A recent report confirms she is sound of mind and she continues to attend church.

Some time after the conference, one of the host pastors was stricken with a serious illness that was compounded by a deep depression. Doctors were confounded by his condition and were giving up hope. When things seemed their darkest, the pastor heard from the Holy Spirit; He told him to pick up the book, *Worship the Lord in Prayer*, to read it, and to live by it. After obeying the counsel of the Holy Spirit, he not only received a complete healing but he also received a better understanding of the importance of praising the Lord. When we revisited Berbice, in November 2009, we were overjoyed to see the increase in their church's praise and worship.

A WORD IN CLOSING

It is my sincerest hope that after reading this book you have come closer to the realization of how truly worthy Jesus is to be praised. In the same way that His love for us is immeasurable, so is the depth of His worthiness. I am thankful that, in the volume of this book, I have been given the opportunity to share with you how very important it is to praise the Lord.

Praising Him is for our wellbeing; it is the key to our freedom. Our praises bring us into His Holy presence; they envelop our prayers and lift them before His Throne of Grace. A priceless pearl begins with a grain. As the oyster covers the grain continually with its secretion, a beautiful pearl emerges. And when we continually cover our prayers with praise, the promises of God are manifested in our lives. It is our continual praise that helps strengthen our confidence, our assured belief, that when we call on His name, His ears are inclined to hear us. It is this confidence that enables us to boldly present our petitions, being mindful to ask each request only once. And it is that confidence that helps us to patiently endure the waiting period that follows.

Inviting Jesus into our hearts is only the first step in getting to know Him. He desires an intimate relationship with each one of us. We should call on His name not only when we have a need, but more importantly, to simply spend time with Him. "But if we walk in the light as He is in the light, we have fellowship with one another, and the blood of Jesus Christ His Son cleanses us from all sin" (1 John 1:7).

Before you close this book, I would like to share a final word of encouragement. The Lord wrote the last three verses of Psalm 91 as a personal declaration to us.

> **Psalm 91:14-16** "Because he has set his love upon Me, therefore I will deliver him; I will set him on high, because he has known My name. He shall call upon Me, and I will answer him; I *will be* with him in trouble; I will deliver him and honor him. With long life I will satisfy him And show him My salvation.

To make the psalm more personal, insert the word *you* wherever you see the pronouns *he*, *his*, and *him* (illustrated below). Keep in mind as you are reading the psalm that the Lord is speaking directly to you.

> Because *you* have set your love upon Me, therefore I will deliver *you*; I will set *you* on high, because *you* have known My name. *You* shall call upon Me, and I will answer *you*; I will be with *you* in trouble; I will deliver *you* and honor *you*. With long life I will satisfy *you* and show *you* My salvation.

His Word is His promise to us. The Word of God is seed. And when that seed is planted in a fertile heart, it *will* take root and our lives *will* bear fruit.

God glorifies Himself by answering our prayers
and we, in turn, glorify Him with the praise of our lips
and testimonies of His goodness towards us.